PHILIP EVERGOOD

PHILIP EVERGOOD

TEXT BY JOHN I. H. BAUR

Director Emeritus, Whitney Museum of American Art, New York

Harry N. Abrams, Inc., Publishers, New York

Frontispiece.
Plate 1. ME AND MY ROSES.
1964. Oil on canvas, 26 x 21".
Collection Amy and Stanley Swerdlow,
Great Neck, New York

Nai Y. Chang, *Vice-President, Design and Production*

John L. Hochmann, *Executive Editor*

Margaret L. Kaplan, *Managing Editor*

Barbara Lyons, *Director, Photo Department, Rights and Reproductions*

Roy Winkler, *Designer*

Library of Congress Cataloging in Publication Data

Baur, John Ireland Howe, 1909-
    Philip Evergood.

    1. Evergood, Philip, 1901-1973   I. Evergood,
Philip, 1901-1973
ND237.E8B32   759.13   72-11790
ISBN 0-8109-0104-8

Library of Congress Catalogue Card Number: 72-11790
Published by Harry N. Abrams, Incorporated, New York, 1975
Printed and bound in Japan

FOREWORD AND ACKNOWLEDGMENTS

The story of Evergood's life is an eventful one, which has not before been told in detail. Much of the present account is in his own words, transcribed from a series of tape-recorded interviews with the author. This technique might easily have inspired a certain self-consciousness, but in Evergood's case no such effect was apparent. What emerged was the spontaneous record of a life, recalled with eloquence, with unusual frankness, and with that innate sense of drama which was so important a part of both his personality and his paintings. Indeed, I doubt if there is another contemporary artist whose life illuminated his art more clearly—not simply because the events of the former are so often reflected in the latter, but also, and more important, because the quality of his response to experience is so nearly identical with the quality of his creative process. It is the nature and intensity of this response which I have tried to preserve in the autobiographical pages drawn from the recordings. All quotations are from the latter unless otherwise noted.

I am most grateful to the artist for the many hours spent on these interviews, for his help in making available a wealth of manuscript and printed material, and for his kindness in permitting me to examine the paintings and drawings in his studio.

The first version of this book was published in 1960 on the occasion of Philip Evergood's retrospective exhibition at the Whitney Museum of American Art, held in the spring of that year. The present version has been expanded to cover work done during the rest of his life; it also has many more illustrations from all periods of his career.

Evergood has been represented by several galleries in New York, all of which were most helpful in providing photographs of works sold and information on their whereabouts. I am particularly indebted to the late Herman Baron of the A.C.A. Gallery and to Mrs. Bella Fishko, now of Forum Gallery but formerly his associate. Terry Dintenfass, Victor J. Hammer, and Lawrence A. Fleischman of Terry Dintenfass, Inc., Hammer Galleries, and Kennedy Galleries, Inc., respectively, were also most helpful, as was Mrs. Joseph James Akston of Gallery 63. The monograph published by the A.C.A. Gallery in 1946 (*20 Years: Evergood*) was an important source of information, as was also the catalogue of Evergood's most recent retrospective exhibition, held at The Gallery of Modern Art in 1969, and Lucy R. Lippard's book, *The Graphic Work of Philip Evergood: Selected Drawings and Complete Prints,* published in 1966.

I am grateful to the late Rosalind Irvine, who prepared the first versions of the chronology and bibliography. Both have been brought up to date, the latter by Mrs. Libby W. Seaberg. I want to extend my special thanks to Mrs. Patricia Westlake for her help in tracing many works to their present owners, assembling the information for the captions, and revising the index.

J.I.H.B.

CONTENTS

LIST OF PLATES

Colorplates are marked with an asterisk (*)

PHILIP EVERGOOD

THE EARLY YEARS

2. LILY AND THE SPARROWS. 1939.
Oil on composition board, 30 x 24″.
Whitney Museum of American Art,
New York City

Philip Evergood was a stocky man endowed with passionate convictions and a voice of astonishing volume. He talked not a little like Gulley Jimson in Joyce Cary's *The Horse's Mouth*—pungently, oratorically, colloquially, dramatically—moving in unpredictable shifts from humor to pathos, from fantasy to hard common sense. He was, above all, an idealist, and his allegiance to causes which won his heart kept him in the frying pan or the fire for much of his life. While the normal laws of consequence can be perceived in some of the disasters that beset him, he himself suspected, not without justification, that a fate intimately entwined in his character attracted trouble as a magnet draws filings. He nearly died twice, in each case through the incredible carelessness of others rather than the illness itself. He was jailed three times, but his most serious brush with the law would never have occurred if a well-meaning prison librarian had not shown reproductions of his work to two young convicts.

As an artist, Evergood has been called a Social Realist, an imaginative Realist, a Surrealist, an Expressionist, and a sophisticated Primitive with a built-in naiveté. "He's as mad as Poe, I sometimes think, but he's also as compelling," Robert Coates once wrote of him. Since the age of four he drew and painted continually. Indeed, he was too prolific for his own good, but this was also a part of his nature, the fruit of an imagination that was probably more active and more uninhibited than any other in twentieth-century American painting. Conventional labels seem inadequate to define an art compounded of so many normally opposed qualities: of fantasy and realism, of sensuousness and satire, of deliberate vulgarity and a fine decorative sensibility, of the acid and the sweet. "Sure I'm a Social Painter," Evergood entitled an article he once wrote for the *Magazine of Art,* but, just as surely, he was unlike any other social painter this country has produced, if only because of that strange and irrational vein which runs through so much of his work. Yet it would be equally misleading to call him a Surrealist or a visionary, for he was not a deliberate wooer of the subconscious, nor was he a mystic. The central fact about his art is that while dealing with life, with everyday experience, it magnifies life to heroic and sometimes fantastic proportions. This magnification by the lens of Evergood's imagination may seem theatrical to some, for it gives to even little truths a wild and intense telling. Others will find it profoundly exhilarating. In either case, it is not a calculated process. It is simply the way one artist thought and felt and saw—one artist who grew fewer protective calluses than most of humanity, who responded completely to the joy and to the agony of living.

Evergood was born Philip Blashki in the studio of his father, Meyer Evergood Blashki, at 118 West 23rd Street, in New York, on October 26, 1901. His grandfather had emigrated from Poland to England, then to Australia where he established a prosperous jewelry business, married, and had fourteen children, of whom Meyer was the last. (Meyer's middle name, Evergood, was a literal translation of his mother's maiden name, Immergut.) Strikingly handsome in the daguerreotypes of him as a youth, Meyer was, from the beginning, restless and a nonconformist. Early in life he disengaged himself from his Orthodox Jewish background, became a painter against the opposition of his father, and for the rest of his life was a rolling stone, seldom settling anywhere for more than a few years at a time. With a friend he painted his way through the South Seas, meeting Stevenson on Samoa, missing Gauguin in Tahiti. For a time he made a precarious living illustrating newspapers in San Francisco. As a painter, he worked in a style of lyrical Impressionism a little like that of Henry Ward Ranger or Gifford Beal, both of whom became his close friends in New York.

Evergood's mother came from a very different background—wealthy, English, gentile. The Perry family traced its origins to the time of the Battle of Hastings. Her grandfather was an Episcopal minister in Falmouth, her father a wealthy businessman who took his daughter with him on his trips to Ceylon, India, China, Japan, and Borneo, buying tea and spices. He had also invested heavily in Australian real estate. It was on a trip to Melbourne in connection with these interests that Flora Jane Perry first met the struggling young artist of Polish descent.

"My mother had had all the advantages of travel and education. She spoke several languages. She was interested in music. A person of great intellect and moral principles—a terrifically courageous person. She met this young artist, Meyer

Blashki, and they fell in love very much. But then he went to San Francisco and she had to go back to England where my grandfather had a big house with beautiful gardens and everything kept up very beautifully. Then, about that time, the Boer War started and my father, who had been an officer in the Australian militia —a sort of Home Guard business—felt it his duty to go to England immediately and join the forces. He was given a horse and was about to go to the war when he looked my mother up, and they found they were still in love. None of the Perrys liked the idea of her marrying a young Australian Jew of Polish descent, a wild-eyed painter who would whisk her off to America. But my father more or less renounced his Jewish background. He was proud of his race, but he never was interested in religion. He wasn't an atheist; he believed in God but he didn't believe in the ceremony of Orthodox Judaism. So they were married at St. Martin-in-the-Fields, which is that big church in Trafalgar Square, in all the style that my grandfather Perry thought fitted his daughter."

Josiah Perry settled $2,500 a year on Flora, and with this modest but dependable income behind them, Meyer Blashki took his bride to New York, gave up his newspaper work, and devoted himself to roaming and painting. He seldom sold a picture and made little effort to do so. Once he wrote to his brother Aaron, who had become a millionaire in the Australian cigar business, asking him to buy a few of his canvases. The return letter, virtually reading him out of the family, made him so angry that he changed his name to Miles Evergood Blashki in a yet further withdrawal from his background. Still, it was possible to live on $2,500 a year in the New York of 1900, and even to manage a trip to Maine in the summer, or to rent a small shack in Connecticut. The studio on 23rd Street was bare but comfortable. Nearby, on 15th Street, Albert Ryder lived like a hermit but admitted them sometimes to the impressive clutter of his studio. Ryder's neighbors, Louise and Charles Fitzpatrick, who cared for him in his final illness, became the Blashkis' closest friends; Evergood remembered Mrs. Fitzpatrick with near veneration as a woman of great warmth and spiritual strength.

As a child, Evergood showed precocious musical ability, which his family encouraged in the hope that he would become a musician. Even before he started his formal education at the Ethical Culture School—indeed, before he was four years old—he began to take piano lessons from a remarkable teacher named Mme. Rabagliatti. The recollection of that experience was more vivid than anything else in his childhood.

"She taught in one of those little studios in the Lincoln Arcade, and she was a very dominant woman. She could bring things out of children that no other person could. I couldn't read a note; she didn't believe in teaching you scales. She was almost like a Svengali. She loved you so and had such force of character that I got so I could go through a piece of Mendelssohn, shall we say, after two or three times, with her playing it and showing me the right way until I could play it too, without any knowledge of music at all. I played—I say it myself—I played magnificently at the age of eight. By nine I really could sit down at the piano and sound like a man playing. I liked it. I thrilled to it. I loved to go and learn a new piece with Mme. Rabagliatti. And then I would come home and practice and cut loose and really emote on that piano. I was so good that when Mme. Rabagliatti put on a concert of her own in one of the smaller halls in Carnegie Hall, I seconded her. I played half the concert and she played half the concert."

When he was eight, Evergood's mother took him to England to be educated, a process that her family was convinced could not be properly achieved in America and for which they were willing to take financial responsibility. Leaving him in a Sussex boarding school, she returned to America, and for the next few years his vacations were spent with his grandmother, who had a pleasant apartment in London, and with other members of the family. A little later his parents both came over and spent several years in a studio in Chelsea.

It was not a happy time in Evergood's life. He ran away from the first school and endured a wretched year at another in Essex. He tried to keep on with his music, but gave up in sheer boredom when he was forced to start at the beginning with scales and reading exercises. The last of his boarding schools was Stubbington House, which specialized in preparing boys for the Royal Naval Training College at Osborne. With music abandoned, his mother had decided that he should become a naval officer. The school was extremely strict, emphasizing mathematics, languages, and geography. Under the pressure of work Evergood's health began to fail and just before his graduation, at the age of thirteen, he was stricken with acute appendicitis. The school matron, apparently suspecting him of malingering, refused to call a doctor and dosed him heavily with Gregory Powder, a violent cathartic. He spent two agonizing days in bed. Then the pain subsided and he managed to graduate and even to take a brief trip with his father to Liverpool. On his return to the Chelsea studio, the pain began again, a doctor was called at three in the morning, and he underwent surgery in a hastily improvised operating room at a nearby nursing home. His appendix had burst, peritonitis had set in, and three more operations were required to drain the poison. When he was released, five months later, he weighed fifty-nine pounds.

"By this time I had heard that I had passed my written examinations for Osborne. But I had also been before a Committee of Admirals, as you had to. They sort of sneered a little about my name—how come with the name of Blashki I wanted to join the British Navy—and now they were holding my admission in abeyance. Of course, with me in this terrible state, the project had to be abandoned anyway, but my father wrote a letter to Winston Churchill, who was then First Lord of the Admiralty, and he put the proposition to him. He said, 'Is it because my son's name is Blashki that this doubt takes place in the minds of the admirals?' And I recall that my father kept the personal, handwritten letter that Churchill wrote him in reply, saying these things shouldn't happen, but they do. The fact that your son's name is Philip Blashki, not Philip Evergood, has an effect on us Anglo-Saxons. I wouldn't be a bit surprised if that is the case here. I would advise you as man to man to change your name legally to Evergood. From Winston Churchill. Not the exact words, but that was the gist of it. And my father, not because of himself but because he felt I don't want my son to be brought up with that to bear all his life, went to a lawyer and had it legally changed."

From then on they were Miles Evergood and Philip Evergood.

Determined that if the British Navy would not have him, her son should go to the best school in England, Evergood's mother announced her intention of entering him at Eton. Though warned of the difficulties of admission, she obtained a personal interview with A. C. G. Heygate, master of one of the houses. To him she told the whole story, including the change of name. Heygate was unexpectedly sympathetic, with the result that Evergood spent the four years of World War I there. It was a rigorous life, rising at six, unheated classrooms, and bare cubicles, but he liked it. The place had an aura of tradition and mystery, he got on well with the other boys, and in Heygate he had an understanding tutor with an uncommon veneration for the arts. Evergood had painted and drawn since he was four, but it was here that he began to let his imagination take him on pictorial journeys through the Bible, the Roman conquests, and the great episodes of history. Some crayon drawings of these years still exist, vivid and fanciful.

"The real reason I am an artist today—I was thinking about this last night—the real reason is that this wonderful man Heygate was a very, very intelligent tutor during the ages when I might have given it up entirely; the difficult age, from fourteen to eighteen. You don't want the discipline of sitting down and learning how to draw academically. You lose your imagination unless you are carried over that period by somebody who inspires you. Heygate and his wife always encouraged me to express my thoughts in drawing; they both would come to my little room at night from time to time and look at the work I'd been doing. They were so keen on art that they even gave a prize, just themselves—a finely bound book or something to inspire their boys to write poetry and paint. In an English school! Most of the people there thought it was terrible to be an artist. 'Oh, it's all right to be an amateur painter, my boy; that's fine, dabble in it, don't you know. But not a serious painter. That's not done.'"

During his last year at Eton, Evergood took officer training for military serv-

3. REACHING FOR THE BLUEBIRD. 1930/46.
Oil on canvas, 56 x 29″.
The Harry N. Abrams Family Collection,
New York City

ice, but the armistice was signed two months before he completed his course. Instead, he graduated and went with a friend to Belgium to be tutored in French, Latin, and mathematics by a Catholic priest, l'Abbé de Moore, a mountainous man who had just been decorated for his daring espionage during the war. Evergood worked hard and spent his spare time in the museums, looking seriously at the old masters—an occupation in which his friends declined to join him. Shortly thereafter he took his competitive examinations for Cambridge University and was admitted to Trinity Hall College.

It soon became apparent that Cambridge was not the place for him. Still unsure of his future career, he rashly tackled a Tripos in English, a degree difficult enough for a scholar and one for which he had neither the capability nor the inclination. He had vague thoughts at this time of taking up law or perhaps civil engineering. He was strongly urged toward the latter course by his uncle, George Stephens Perry, who had already been honored by the Khedive of Egypt for his brilliant work in heightening the Aswan Dam, then the largest structure of its kind in the world, and who offered to train him and make him his assistant. Meanwhile Evergood drifted, spending too little time on his studies, too much time rowing on the river. Occasionally he would wander into the Fitzwilliam Museum to look at paintings, and these were the best moments. In the fall of 1921, soon after he had started his second year at Cambridge, the realization swept over him that he did not want to be a lawyer, a scholar, or an engineer, that the one thing he felt in his bones he could do was be an artist. There remained the problem of persuading his family, though in this he had the unexpected support of Henry Bond, Trinity Hall's head. Even so, it was not easy.

"It was hard, terribly hard. My uncle, George Perry, had just at that time married a French countess, Countess Céline de Brie. I think she came from the part of France where they make the cheeses. In any case she, George, and I had a big conference when I told them that I felt I ought to leave Cambridge and go in for art, that art was the only thing I had in my veins, inherited from my father, and that I might make a go of it. Céline, being a Frenchwoman, felt that she had all the tradition and background. She knew the work of Cézanne, Gauguin, and Corot. She felt that the great culture in painting was France, only France. She said, 'Frankly, my dear boy, you haven't got any talent for painting at all.' George and she became so upset by the whole argument that they finally sort of took their support away from me and practically said, 'If you want to leave Cambridge it's your own headache; you'll have to make out the best way you can.'

"So I went to Bond, a beautiful old man of eighty at the time, sitting at his desk in the wonderful, monastic atmosphere of his quarters. He opened the door as though he was ushering in a dear friend, and said, 'Sit down, my dear boy, and we'll talk this thing out. I have looked over your reports and even studied some of your papers. I don't think you have really got a grasp of your subject to the extent that we are demanding it of you. You are more in the creative field, I suspect. If you have this impulse and desire to go in for art, by jove, why don't you? I'll back you up. Henry Tonks, the head of the Slade School, is a dear friend of mine. I will write him a letter. Take your work to him. Don't be afraid. Go, and I'll make it right with your parents and your relatives.'

"So I got on a train, went to London, and my father put in his two-cents-worth. He said, 'You know, my son, I've been through the agonies of the damned as a painter and never had any recognition. I've never sold my work. You're going to have a terrible struggle. I don't feel you should do it, but I'll help all I can.' "

Tonks had a reputation for ferocity and inaccessibility. On his father's recommendation, Evergood went first to Havard Thomas, a stout and genial sculptor who had excavated at Pompeii and was a distinguished expert on ancient methods of casting. He was then head of the sculpture department at the Slade, while Tonks directed the department of painting and drawing. Thomas looked at the nervous young artist's drawings, reassured him warmly, and suggested they go to Tonks at once.

"So he took me up on the top of a bus. I'll never forget that ride with that wonderful old man. He looked something like Balzac, little moustache and a round pink-and-white face. He took me to Tonks, went in to talk to Tonks, came out, and I was waiting outside, and he said, 'Go in to the great man,' and I went in. I was trembling all over, and I opened my portfolio and showed the drawings to Tonks. I'd been told that you had to have a few things from life, so I had drawn a picture of my own hands and brought a few drawings I had made of my mother, as careful as I could, in addition to some of my Biblical things. Tonks looked at them all. He said, 'My boy, you can't draw. You cannot draw; get that into your head.' He was a tall, thin man, about six-foot-three, I would say, with an acid wit. He never cracked a smile, but you always felt he was smiling behind those eyes.

"He said, 'Look, if you want to go in for art, don't feel you're going to make money at it. If you want to make money, go into something else—not art. You're going into a religion. You're going to be a priest in a religion. You're going to starve, you're going to be battered around, you're going to be disliked—because you're an artist. You are not going to get recognition. You're going to be struggling in a little room for bread most of your life, and if you are lucky you may make a few pennies out of your art at the end of your life. Remember that. Otherwise I don't want you here.'

"I was so relieved that I was overwhelmed with happiness. 'I absolutely feel the same way,' I told him. 'My father is a painter. We've struggled. It seems to me it is the only thing I'm cut out for.'

"He said, 'You cannot draw, but your drawings did something to me that few do, which is a good thing. They made me laugh. I will take you at the Slade.'"

Evergood began his studies the same day, and for two years he went through the rigorous academic training that Tonks imposed, drawing, always drawing. The pencil had to be sharpened to a pinpoint, the lead extending a full half inch. The point was used for contours and details, the side of the lead for shading, which must be laid on in a systematic diagonal, from right to left. The shading also served to renew the sharpness of the point. Alternately drawing and shading, a skillful draftsman could often complete a drawing without resharpening his pencil. Evergood did no painting at the Slade, but he studied sculpture with Havard Thomas, and in his spare time made a little money assisting him in his studio. With a small monthly allowance from his mother, he got by. At the end of two years he had won his certificate in drawing.

In the summer of 1922, before he left the Slade, Evergood made a brief trip to America to help settle his parents, who had decided to return there permanently. On his graduation in 1923, he felt a sudden conviction that despite his long years in England, America was his native country. He had been traveling on a British passport, but he wrote to the State Department in Washington, which confirmed his American citizenship, and he was issued an American passport. He then rejoined his family in New York and continued his studies for a year at the Art Students League, where he worked with William von Schlegell and George Luks. Luks tried to persuade him to paint, but Evergood felt he needed a still firmer foundation in drawing and resisted the temptation. Often he sketched at night at the Educational Alliance school and did a little painting on his own. Two friends, Philip Reisman and Harry Sternberg, taught him to etch and let him use their press.

Unfortunately, friction developed at home. Evergood, now twenty-two, had lived little with his family since the age of eight. His mother was not well (the cancer which would kill her in three years was beginning its wasting inroads), and both he and his father had strong temperaments.

"I was a man by then and it was hard to live with the very strong and fiery disposition of my father, who was constantly sneering and swearing at me because he wasn't sure that I was doing as good work as I should and because he was a different age and didn't understand some of my experiments. He felt I was becoming a waster and a playboy instead of disciplining myself, and we had terrible fights. I can remember him criticizing an etching plate I was working on and I hurled it across the room and it stuck in the wall. Then I rushed out of the house, just in my undershirt and pants, and roamed through New York all night.

"My mother sensed that we needed a change, so she called up Melville Chater, a writer friend who was about to go on another one of his canoe trips through Europe for the *National Geographic Magazine*. She said, 'We are having a terrible time here in the home. Phil is not able to work, he is coming into conflict all the time with his father. Could he be of any use helping you over to Europe with the canoe? I will give him $50 or $60 a month and any money that you can give to help along will be fine.' So he said, 'Good. I'll pay his expenses over, to help me paddle the canoe through Europe.' So I accompanied him.

"Before the end of that trip he and I were at each other's throats like cat and dog. He felt I hadn't done enough work on the trip, that I had been lazy, and I had, too. There were too many distractions for me to sit down at every little stop and sketch. In the evenings he expected me to take my painting materials and go out and paint three or four paintings. We had a big showdown fight in Ostend. He took his canoe and said, 'To hell with you. Go to Paris and do what you want to.' So we separated. I went off to Paris and he went up the Rhine with his canoe. That's how I got to Paris, began to make my own way, learned a little colloquial French, enough to get around the studios, and started to paint seriously."

Like so many young Americans, Evergood enrolled in the Académie Julian, but when he discovered that the criticism by Laurens consisted of a weekly walk around the studio, a few casual remarks, and a polite departure, he left. For a brief time he worked with André Lhote, but did not take to the rigid rules of composition Lhote imposed on his class. For the most part he worked independently in the big pleasant room overlooking a courtyard which he had found in the Rue du Cherche-Midi. His self-training as a painter really began here, with a series of still lifes meticulously studied and brushed. Occasionally he would hire a model with friends and work from the figure.

Soon he began to meet other artists and writers: Utrillo, Pascin, Signac, Bourdelle, Foujita, Man Ray, and Eugene O'Neill. Two of his closest friends were a painter named Hiddingh and a young architect, McNeil Siple. Their passionate discussions of art, from El Greco to Van Gogh, did much to fill in his background of art history. He was also deeply interested in the work of the Cubists and the Surrealists, although not himself much drawn in either of those directions.

"But I always have taken my hat off to what they have done because you've got to be sensitive to whatever brains in your own age are thinking about. You've got to give them credit for having brains."

Through Hiddingh he met his future wife, Julia Cross, who had worked for five years in a Wall Street office to save enough money to study ballet in Paris and who was later to become a fine dancer, appearing with Mordkin and Volonine, with the Ballet Russe of Monte Carlo, and in recitals of her own. It was not until later that he saw much of her, however. Now, after a year of Paris, he began to travel, going first

4. M. T. FLORINSKY, D. S. MIRSKY AND THE PIDGET. 1928 (slightly enlarged c. 1945).
Oil on canvas, 41 x 51″. Collection Michael T. Florinsky, Vevey, Switzerland

to Italy where he visited Milan and Venice, spending several months in Florence, and eventually working his way down to Naples. On the way back he stopped at Rome and studied for about six weeks at the British Academy. But he felt Rome was a city for sculptors; he could see the ghosts of the great ones walking its streets, while the ghosts of the painters stayed in Florence. From Italy he went to the tiny village of Cagnes in the south of France for several months, and rented a studio from a certain Mme. Rosalie.

"She was a wonderful woman, a great friend of Suzanne Valadon, Utrillo's mother; her own son was supposed to be the illegitimate child of Whistler. I had been to her restaurant in Paris and got to know her. She was awfully nice to me. She and her son lived underneath the little studio room she rented to me. Utrillo would visit them and sleep downstairs in the kitchen. They had great crocks of wine and we would all sit around the fire drinking wine, with her son playing his guitar. I painted the son. It was quite a good picture, but I got mad with it years later and destroyed it."

In 1926 Evergood returned to America to be near his mother, whose health was failing badly. A family friend, the author Harvey O'Higgins, lent him a studio in Martinsville, New Jersey, and there he continued to paint, working especially on a series of classical Biblical scenes. Early in 1927 he took a group of these and other pictures to the Dudensing Gallery in New York, which was planning to feature young American artists. To his delight he was accepted and promised a show, his first one-man exhibition, in the fall. Even before it opened Murdock Pemberton, art critic of *The New Yorker,* saw several of his things and wrote, "He is immensely facile. He can paint like every good painter you have come across. . . . Eventually he will be full of guts and, we hope, of Evergood."

When the exhibition opened in November, the reviews were generally favorable, though nearly every critic noted the strong influence of El Greco and Cézanne. Judging by the few surviving canvases of this period, it is true that little of the artist's personal note had emerged. Yet it was about to. The following summer, on a visit to Woodstock, N.Y., Evergood painted the fanciful double portrait, *M. T. Florinsky, D. S. Mirsky and the Pidget* (plate 4). The two Russian emigrés, so different in appearance and (according to the artist) in their views, sit on a magic carpet, while behind them are spread the symbols of their past in imperial Russia. Among other things, they are discussing a dream of Florinsky's in which he encountered a strange animal, half pigeon, half rabbit. While they are talking, the Pidget himself materializes and joins the conversation. Although the picture was enlarged at a much later date, and the feet then added, the central portion remains virtually unchanged and shows that naive directness of drawing and characterization that was to become a hallmark of Evergood's mature work. The fantasy of the whole concept also forecasts another element in his art which was not to develop fully for several years, although there are traces of it in *Solomon at the Court of Sheba* (plate 39), which he painted a little later.

After another one-man exhibition, at the Montross Gallery in 1929, Evergood returned to France. His mother had died two years earlier, dissolving the bond that tied him most strongly to America. He had sold a few pictures, saved a little money, and was further impelled to leave New York by an unhappy love affair which was destroying his peace of mind and making it impossible for him to paint. In Paris he found a studio in the Rue Delambre and gradually regained his equilibrium. To support himself he built stage scenery for a theater, worked as a carpenter on some exposition buildings, and as a sparring partner for professional boxers. He studied briefly with William Hayter at Atelier 17 to learn something of engraving, but for the most part he painted independently. He also fell in love with Julia Cross, who was now dancing for Volonine and working part time for Caresse Crosby's Black Sun Press.

"I was very much in love with her. I intended to marry her but I didn't want to take her away from her dancing. She had this terrific ambition to become a great dancer. She was one of the best in Volonine's ballet group, working day and night with him. And I persuaded her to run away to Spain with me. We got in a third-class carriage. We had no money. We went down to Spain just as King Alfonso was coming out; the country was in turmoil; foreigners were endangering their lives by going there at that time. People were killed on the streets, guns were going off all the time, and we—two little artists—we got down to Toledo through Madrid with all the excitement, reached Toledo, and ended up just by accident in a little apartment overlooking El Greco's garden.

"I think El Greco impressed me, when I saw him in Spain, more than anything has ever impressed me—the terrific fluidity of his painting. It looks as if the paint had been blown on, as if it had just flown on the canvas by itself. This is what hit me and made me realize that painting was not what Michelangelo did in the Sistine Chapel—that's just drawing filled·in with color—but that painting was plastic, the liquid color put on the surface in a way that gives depth, movement, and spiritual values and expression to a face. What wonderful expressions of faces in all this swiftly flowing handling of the paint!

"I've always felt that if a man could draw like Dürer or Cranach or some of those wire-lined, precise draftsmen and then loosen up, he would be going in the direction of Greco and the great painters. You can't be a virtuoso of paint when you're young. If you do, it all goes into mush, like Sorolla. In Greco the discipline is always there under the surface. But the handling is like the fluttering of angels' wings. I think others have come near to it. Some of Pascin's little feathery pencil

5. NUDE BY THE EL. 1934. Oil on canvas, 37⅜ x 42⅞". Hirshhorn Museum and Sculpture Garden, Smithsonian Institution, Washington, D.C.

lines filled in with a divine pink and delicate pale white for the skin come mighty near it sometimes—but you can't compare the two. One is a monument of a man and the other is a sensitive man."

Soon Julia Cross returned to America, Evergood to Paris. But much of the magic and excitement seemed to have gone out of the French capital. He did not wish to be an expatriate painter. And while he had not yet formed any program of painting the American scene, a conviction grew that he wanted to develop, as an artist, in the atmosphere of his own country. On the spur of the moment, he one day rolled up his canvases, bought a boat ticket, and came back to New York. He did not go abroad again.

He was hardly off the boat when he and Julia were married. The year was 1931, the economic depression was deepening, and they had almost no money. None of the government art projects had as yet been started, and painters—even those with established reputations—were among the first to suffer. For a young artist just embarking on his career, the situation was close to desperate, but Mrs. Cross, Julia's mother, came to the rescue. She was then working for Miss Amelia White in a gallery of American Indian art on Madison Avenue, and she hired her daughter as a bookkeeper and Evergood as a part-time handyman to build shelves and mount displays. Their respective salaries were $25 and $20 a week, but it kept them going and gave Evergood some time to paint. The Montross Gallery again took him on, giving him one-man shows in 1933 and 1935, from which a few canvases were sold. In that second year he won the Kohnstamm Prize at the Art Institute of Chicago with *Evening Reading* and accepted an invitation to join the Midtown Gallery group. In 1937 he made a signal switch of dealers when he went to the A.C.A. Gallery, which was then over the Village Barn on 8th Street. In its director, Herman Baron, he found a deeply sympathetic supporter whose understanding and devotion to his work played a major role in accomplishing his recognition as an artist.

These were the truly formative years in the development of Evergood's mature style. He began to lose interest in purely imaginative subjects, such as his Biblical scenes, and in studio paintings of still lifes and nudes. Instead, he began to draw more directly on his own life and experiences. If he now hired a model, as he did for *Nude by the El* (plate 5), she became only one element in a modern conversation piece which embraced his family and friends, his Milligan Place apartment, and a little drama of workmen peering through the window. Several canvases are frankly storytelling ones. *Burial of the Queen of Sheba* (plate 6) recounts the pathetic (and illegal) internment of their cat in a neighboring backyard, which he and his wife reached by scaling a wall at night. *Evening Reading* (plate 41) is the record of a visit to his studio by two friends, Charles Edward Smith, poet and an expert on the history of jazz, and his wife Louise, daughter of the painter Kenneth Hayes Miller; so strong is its sense of intimacy that it scandalized several conservative viewers in Chicago. While both these paintings might be called autobiographical, the range of Evergood's sympathies soon expanded to embrace humanity on a wider stage.

"I think one of the things I saw that probably drove me faster into this way of thinking was on a cold winter night when I went out for a walk down Christopher Street toward the North River. It was about ten o'clock. I passed the post office and government building at the end of the street and came to a big empty lot with about fifty little shacks on it, all made out of old tin cans, crates, orange boxes, mattresses for roofs. Most of them were not even as tall as a man; you would have to crawl in on hands and knees. Snow was on the ground, a fire was lit, and a group of Negroes and white men were huddled around the fire. These were the outcasts of New York, the outcasts of civilization. The only food they had was from garbage cans, the only fire they had was from sticks they picked up around the wharves.

"I went over to the fire and talked to them. They didn't seem to resent me, and I felt that they were all very cold so I went through my pockets and brought out two or three dollars and told them to go and get some gin. They bought a big bottle and all had a drink and warmed themselves up. We sat around the fire and talked. They couldn't call themselves by ordinary names—Old Foot was one, Terrapin another. They were interesting people, but their tragedy hit me between the eyes because I had never been as close to anything like that before.

"Then I got a brain wave. It seemed to me that I should be involved in my work with this kind of thing. So I walked to 49 Seventh Avenue, where we lived, and got some drawing materials and came back and sat with them and drew them all night until dawn. I used some of those drawings later for paintings I did on the WPA."

Evergood's rising awareness of human drama as material for his art also sprang, to some extent, from his admiration of John Sloan's work and from his close personal friendship with that pioneer of urban realism. Sloan, with characteristic generosity, was enthusiastic about the young man's work, seeing him as the inheritor of his own warm and humorous appreciation of the city's teeming life. Several of Evergood's early pictures were in a similar vein, though not much related to Sloan's work stylistically. *Dance Marathon* captured the tawdry glitter of its subject. *Treadmill* (plate 42) commented on the frank exposure of physical charms by the maidens of 14th Street, exaggerated by rendering their dresses transparent (a device, incidentally, which George Grosz had used in his Berlin drawings, though Evergood was not aware of it at the time). *The Siding* (plate 45) recorded an actual scene which had caught Evergood's eye as he was driving on Cape Cod one day; even the fanciful handcar actually existed, although the fantasy is surely heightened in the painting. *Art on the Beach* and *Street Corner* (plates 7, 44) were crowded panoramas of life in Provincetown and New York respectively, overflowing with comic incidents and minor dramas, very much in the spirit of Bruegel.

In all of these works—both the autobiographical canvases and those of the larger scene—Evergood's distinctive style may be seen evolving. He had looked long, as he has often acknowledged, at the paintings of Grünewald, Bruegel, Bosch, and El Greco, the graphic work of Goya, Daumier, and Toulouse-Lautrec, at cave painting, at child art, and the movies of Charlie Chaplin. All of these influences, and others less obvious, entered into the formation of his own art. Perhaps its most striking characteristic at this time was the deliberate awkwardness of the drawing, sometimes veering toward satire but more often suggesting the spontaneous expressiveness of primitive painting—a line that probes for the bold, essential contour, the telling gesture, and surrounds these triumphantly, without any stylish flourishes or sinuosities of its own. The gaiety of the little boats in *Art on the Beach* and the pathos of the grotesque cat in *Burial of the Queen of Sheba* (plate 6) indicate something of the emotional range which this calculated naiveté of handling could produce, particularly in contrast to the sophisticated designs and the skillful organization of the many figures.

Other emergent elements, which were to become important in his later work, were his uses of symbolism, space, and color. The first hardly needs to be dwelt on, for it is never abstruse or mystical. When it occurs its meaning is clear enough, like the cobweb-patterned floor in *Dance Marathon* (plate 40), which seems to trap the weary dancers in its meshes. Evergood's spatial sense is more complicated. From the beginning he shunned any illusion of great depth, and he has always preferred to organize his forms on a shallow stage rigorously tied to the plane of the canvas. This is obvious in *Treadmill,* which is virtually a frieze, but it is also apparent in pictures of superficially deeper perspective. *Nude by the El* (plate 5) seems almost Cubist-inspired in the way floor and couch are tipped toward the spectator, while the far view is effectively blocked off by the insistent treatment of the window mullions. In more elaborate compositions, such as *Art on the Beach* and *Street Corner,* the artist's insistence on this shallow space results in a violent compression of the many figures, somewhat akin to that of Tintoretto, El Greco, and Mannerist art. This compression has its emotional as well as its purely aesthetic uses; it lends itself to a kind of concentrated violence of both feeling and design.

Some of the same violence is apparent in Evergood's early color, which often clashes in raucous disharmonies of reds and oranges and pulsating electric blues—

6. **BURIAL OF THE QUEEN OF SHEBA.** 1933. Oil on canvas, 22 x 28".
Bernard Danenberg Galleries, New York City

7. ART ON THE BEACH. c. 1936. Oil on canvas, 35½ x 51¼".
National Gallery of Victoria, Melbourne, Australia

the dominant scheme in several canvases of the thirties. Later he was to become both more subtle and more varied, with an instinctive feeling for unusual color combinations which would be expressive of each picture's mood. He has never resorted to conventional harmonies, with the result that his color is, to many spectators, an acquired taste. It is also among the most personal elements in his art, and one which had its birth during these early years.

"I have an idea that my beginnings of finding myself in color came at about the time I painted *Nude by the El*. I was really pleased with the nasty red in relation to other colors in the painting. It could only be nasty—any color can only be nasty or nice—in relation to something else, right? I felt really thrilled and pleased with the violent reds of the velvet couch the model is lying on in relation to the paleness of her skin and the rather crude house-paint green on the elevated structure outside and the pinks on the wall and the yellows in the mirror. It seemed to me that I had struck a note that I liked very much, one that got away from an everything-is-beautiful-beautiful harmony. It gave me a little shot in the arm to have painted that way once, and I found it going into other canvases where it seemed to develop as a kind of curious taste which very few people liked, and like, but it pleases me for some reason."

When Mrs. Cross died, the Indian gallery, which had supported Evergood and his wife since their marriage, was discontinued. Fortunately the Public Works of Art Project had been founded in 1933, and early in the following year it took Evergood on its rolls. He worked for this and for its successor, the Federal Art Project of the WPA, until about 1937. These were the years of his most militant social propaganda in painting and of his deepest personal involvement in a variety of liberal and even radical causes, which his idealism impelled him to support. He was an early member of the Artists Committee of Action and a president of the Artists Union, into which it grew. He signed the call for the American Artists Congress and was active in its affairs. He took part in movements in behalf of Negro rights, the Spanish Loyalist cause, and Russian War relief. As Managing Supervisor of the Federal Art Project's Easel Division, he fought aggressively to keep good artists on its rolls at a time when it was their only possible means of support. He was arrested in Hoboken for sketching the slums. He was arrested in New York for taking part in the "219 Strike," when 219 artists invaded the WPA offices to protest layoffs from the Project. Behind all these activities lay a deep devotion to democratic and egalitarian ideals, not always wisely acted on, but acted on with courage and the conviction that the artist could not stand aloof from the suffering and struggles of his times.

"When I thought of my background of Eton and Cambridge and that kind of nonsense, which had taken up so much of my life (but which had its value, I think), I felt very moved to shake it off and to be a part of what I was painting, the way Daumier and Courbet and Goya were. It was a feeling that you have to know humanity at the time you live. You can't just sit down at a desk and write a *Nana* unless you've lived it, by God, unless you've damn well sat in a cold basement half the night with down-and-outers and felt their suffering. And to me it meant even more. It meant fighting for them politically, besides putting it down on canvas. It meant sacrificing your good comfortable safety to fight for some of these guys and stick my neck out too.

"So I got into things like the 219 sit-in strike to defend artists on the WPA. I was one of the smaller organizers. Paul Bloch, the sculptor who was killed in Spain a short time later, was the really brave man and conspicuously the revolutionary leader of it, you might say. He stuck his chin right out and put his arms right around that post and they had to beat him insensible to get him out of there. They beat me insensible, but just because I was standing in the front line and refused to ungrip my arms with the others around me, and refused to leave the building. My nose was broken, blood was pouring out of my eyes, my ear was all torn down, my overcoat had been taken, and the collar ripped off. I was pushed out by the police at the bottom of the elevator and thrown into a Black Maria. Later they took us to a vile jail up on the West Side, and they put us in cells where the toilets had overflowed and we were standing, ankle-deep, men and women, all night in that filth. We were tried *en masse,* and escaped with a warning.

"Perhaps I overdid the action—not because my convictions aren't the same now as then—but maybe I could have done just as much by putting the time into my work. Still, what's lost on action may be gained in feeling. This is putting it a little crudely, or rather too simply, but I don't think that anybody who hasn't been really beaten up by the police badly, as I have, could have painted an *American Tragedy."*

American Tragedy (plate 47), like so many of Evergood's works, is based on a specific incident, in this case a bloody battle between picketing strikers and police which took place outside a steel mill in Chicago, on Memorial Day, 1937. It was painted in part from newspaper photographs. (Evergood has often used newspapers, magazines, seed and mail-order catalogues because he finds in them a peculiarly American flavor.) But, needless to say, the picture is essentially a product of his own imagination which soared on this occasion into a realm of theatrical heroism and villainy. The defiant worker protecting his pregnant wife, the fragile straw bonnet about to be trodden into the dust, the brutal faces of the police, the pathetic ones of the fallen strikers, push the picture perilously close to the boundary between art and propaganda. It is saved not only by the quality of the painting —the strong, harsh drawing, the vibrating design—but also, paradoxically, by the very violence of the conception, which raises the picture to a symbol of tragic social strife rather than a comment on a specific instance of it. Nevertheless, there is still an artistic danger involved in a symbolism that deals so exclusively in black-and-white values. Like *East Lynne* and other morality plays of a past era, it must face the prospect of a different reception when the passions which inspired it have cooled and the social problem it dealt with has changed.

All of Evergood's more militant social paintings of the 1930s run this danger and escape it with varying degrees of success. *Mine Disaster* (plate 49), a somber and moving picture in its left and central sections, might have been more powerful without the stressed pathos of the woman and children at the right. The artist is at his best when he tempers tragedy with acid wit and the irrepressible exuberance which are so much a part of his nature. *The Pink Dismissal Slip* (plate 50) with its grotesquely beefy artist, its wonderfully evoked tenement atmosphere, and its sense of the separateness of human lives, embodied in the woman climbing the stairs, is, like life itself, both sad and funny. *Through the Mill* (plate 8), though it details the drudgery of factory work in the vignettes glimpsed through every one of the forty-odd windows, is a picture of such human warmth, buoyancy, and humor—and of such essential truth to the American scene—that it wakes a nostalgia today for those vanishing New England mill towns which were nearly beautiful in their ugliness.

In several paintings the social significance is implied rather than stated, and the focus is on the individual rather than the mass. *Turmoil* (plate 65) opposes a De Chirico-like background of lonely factories to a woman whose defiance and longing are written in every line of face and body. Despite the starkness of the design, unusual for Evergood, it is a psychologically subtle painting with a strong undercurrent of sexual desire. *Lily and the Sparrows* (plate 2) might also be called a psychological portrait, though here the contrast of the head with the extreme realism of the setting creates a dreamlike impression of fantasy, a note which was to be sounded more frequently in Evergood's work of later years. Lily was no dream, however. Nor was the waxen face born entirely of his imagination, though perhaps only Evergood would have seen it thus and none but Evergood would have labored so long for precisely that expression.

"I was walking along that section under the old El, between 6th Street and West Broadway, in a sort of a dream, thinking of something else, and I happened to stop at the curb, just dreaming, and look up, and here was an amazing sight. A little, bald-headed, white beautiful face was in a window with little bits of crumbs—alone. Mother out to work probably, father maybe in the hospital. She could have fallen out and been killed. There she was, leaning out of the window and looking up, and there were a couple of little sparrows flying around in the air. She was feeding

8. THROUGH THE MILL. 1940. Oil and tempera on canvas, 36 x 52".
Whitney Museum of American Art, New York City

them. I thought to myself, my God, this is it, this tells the story and I've been given this just for standing here.

"I was invited to show at the Whitney Museum a little later, and I decided to send this picture. But the night before it was due I was still working on it. I must have painted fifty faces, one over the other, to get what I wanted. I looked at the picture just as I was about to put it in the frame to deliver next morning, and it seemed to have gotten more doll-like and less human the more I worked on it. Suddenly something came over me and I said, to hell with it, I'll scrape it off and repaint the face tonight. So I grabbed my palette knife. The paint had not thoroughly dried, even with all the coats of a month or two. I said, boy, you've got to have courage here, and I slashed off all the coats of paint on the face, and I looked at it—and it was perfect. I'd uncovered a series of layers, and all the various expressions that I'd gotten had amalgamated. All I had to do was to blow on a little retouching varnish to freshen it up, and it all became one, like one beautiful thing under one skin. In a clumsier way, I did what Leonardo did in a brainy way with his *Mona Lisa*. He painted fifty smiles on the one canvas and blended them all into the most divine smile in the world. I did it by accident."

Throughout his life, facial expression, that fleeting, mysterious mirror of mood and character, played a larger role in Evergood's work than in that of most contemporary painters, except perhaps for a few like Jack Levine.

THEMES AND DEVELOPMENT

Evergood's reputation grew steadily in the 1930s. Oddly enough, his first widespread recognition came as a mural painter, although he did relatively little work in this field. In 1932, however, an uncommissioned sketch for a mural and one finished panel of it (repainted many years later as *Artist's Fantasy*) were exhibited at the Museum of Modern Art, where they won favorable notice. Perhaps on the basis of this, the WPA assigned Evergood in 1936 to the Mural Section of the Federal Art Project and gave him 150 square feet of wall to decorate in the public library at Richmond Hill, New York. The founding of this Utopian garden community in 1870 by Albon Platt Man and a group of associates gave Evergood a congenial subject, which he handled symbolically with much ingenuity and imagination (plate 9). Dividing his long narrow space into three sections by means of a painted door and a fragment of wall, around and through which the action flows with unimpeded vigor, he portrayed the founders in the center, the rural joys of their community at the left, and the slums which they were bent on abolishing at the right. His natural preference for a shallow space, organized strongly in the plane of the picture, was well adapted to mural work. His painting holds to the wall despite the activeness of the design and the exuberant wealth of incident and detail. Few murals of the period have stood up so well in vitality and interest.

Unfortunately these qualities were lost on a good part of the conservative Richmond Hill populace. Criticisms began early in 1937, while the paint was still wet. In response to these, Evergood made a few minor changes. In the fall of the same year the mural was completed and was strongly endorsed by Ernest Peixotto, chairman of the Municipal Art Commission. This did nothing, however, to still the popular clamor. The granddaughter of a founder claimed the mural had brought her to the verge of apoplexy. The figures were accused of looking like Russian peasants of the worst sort or, alternately, of not looking like human beings at all. A minister was reported to have complained bitterly of "the emphasis on the mammary glands." The Queens Borough Library Board voted to remove the mural, which aroused a counterstorm of protest from artists, critics, and the heads of the Federal Art Project. Finally, in late May, 1938, the library board reversed itself and officially accepted the mural. The long controversy was over.

Evergood painted two other murals, neither of them as successful as *The Story of Richmond Hill*. One, *Cotton from Field to Mill* (plate 56), was done just a year later (1938) for the U. S. Post Office in Jackson, Georgia. Commissioned by the Section of Fine Arts of the Treasury Department, it ran into nearly as much local opposition as the Richmond Hill painting. Numerous changes were forced on the artist (including the substitution of three small bushes in the foreground for a woman suckling her child), and the installation of the canvas was held up interminably. More important is the fact that Evergood himself does not seem to have been much inspired by his subject. The semicircular design is pedestrian, and the figures lack the expressive vitality of his best work. It is a highly competent decoration, but not much more. His last mural, started two years later, is better. This is *The Bridge of Life* at Kalamazoo College, Michigan, where he was resident artist from 1940 to 1942. Though the subject is a conventional one and verges on the oversweet, the Renaissance-inspired design is more interesting and is well adapted to the vaulted space. Unfortunately the execution was delayed by a serious illness which kept him off the scaffold for several months and he did not have time to finish the area at the right with the care he wished.

During these same years, Evergood's easel paintings began to reach a wider public through various museum exhibitions. The Whitney Museum of American Art showed his *Art on the Beach* (plate 7) in 1934 and included him in many of its subsequent Annuals. The Art Institute of Chicago hung his work in 1935. The Denver Art Museum gave him a one-man show in 1936. The Athenaeum Gallery in Melbourne, Australia, mounted a two-man exhibition in 1937 of paintings by Evergood and his father (who had long since returned to his native country, where he was to die the following year); *Life* magazine reported a record attendance and bitter fights between academicians and modernists, but the latter raised enough

Evergood and student assistants working on the mural
THE BRIDGE OF LIFE, at Kalamazoo College, Michigan, 1940

10. THE JESTER. 1950. Oil on canvas, 72 x 96".
Whitney Museum of American Art, New York City.
Gift of Sol Brody (subject to life interest)

money by subscription to purchase *Art on the Beach* for Melbourne's National Gallery of Victoria. By 1938 Evergood had shown in the Carnegie International at Pittsburgh, and from 1940 on his name appeared in virtually every important annual and biennial in the country. His reputation was established.

Then came, simultaneously, two blows of fate which were not without effect on certain aspects of his art. It was the summer of 1941. He and Julia were vacationing on Cape Cod after their first year at Kalamazoo College.

"Julie was pregnant. She'd given up everything, given up her dancing, sat waiting for this child to grow inside her. She'd go out into the garden and play her castanets. She had always longed for a child. It was the happiest time of our life. I was working, painting all the time. It was an important period in my existence. But then she would come in from outside and find me asleep, lying in front of my easel. She'd shake me and I'd wake up, but I was in a sort of autointoxication. I was being poisoned by something. This went on until finally I went to a very fine diagnostician in Boston who X-rayed me and told me that I had a very serious obstruction of the intestine. The passage was only one half inch and was closing by the hour. I must be operated on within two days.

"So I had to go home, to our little cottage where Julie was waiting, and break the news that this very serious operation had to be done—a resection of the colon. Julie came back to Boston with me and took a hotel room. They got the finest surgeon in America to operate. Great surgeon. I went into the operation, came out, and this great surgeon told Julie it was cancer, malignant, but I wasn't to know. Fortunately he cleared it all out. Eight weeks later I was still running a temperature. The great surgeon had gone away to write a paper on something, and the assistant surgeon, who was also very fine, but a young man, got worried. They X-rayed my brain and my lungs several times, thinking it might be a tubercular infection or something, but found nothing. So in desperation one day the young surgeon came in, and he said, 'Evergood, you've got to go down to the X-ray room; we're going to X-ray your belly this time.' So they put this great big machine over my abdomen, and I was still lying under it when the woman came out of the developing room. She was white. She called up the head of the nurses, and they all trooped in and doctors came in and looked at me as if I was some kind of a freak. She showed them the X-ray plate, and it had a metal plate with a number 22 on it. They had left in my abdomen the pillow, not a sponge but the original surgical pillow, mind you, that they put in to raise the intestines to operate.

"So then of course the great surgeon rushed back. Peritonitis had set in and the whole damn section, where the pillow was, was all rotted. And the whole bloody operation had to be done all over again. I was in the hospital four months in all, and during that time Julie used to come every day and sit with me and read to me with a smile on her face and this child developing inside her. Then, while I was recovering after the second operation, she disappeared for a week, which worried me quite a bit. Finally I learned she had had a miscarriage with the shock of it all. She lost the child and couldn't have another. Our whole lives would have been different if that hadn't happened—just that little accident."

When Evergood was released, he painted a picture charged with hate—the young surgeon leaning over the foot of his bed, frightened and belligerent, trying to explain the incredible error, and beyond him the view of Boston that was stamped on the artist's memory from his long months of lying and watching it. Fifteen years later he painted out the figure, feeling that the rawness of emotion it expressed was overviolent, and substituted for it the profile of a merchant seaman whom he had seen at the hospital convalescing from burns. The painting is now *Snug Harbor* (plate 11). A more oblique but also a more poignant expression of the sadness that filled his life at this time is the wraithlike vision of *Juju as a Wave* (plate 60), a picture which he had completed in 1935 as a joyful tribute to his wife's dedication as a dancer, but which he now repainted, softening all the details of the anatomy, half dissolving the figure into the mysterious blue-grays of the background, and giving the face a tragic expression, remote and ethereal. For this one moment he turned aside from the main direction of his art and entered the visionary, twilight world of Blake and Ryder. He revisited it seldom and nearly always in a spirit of sadness. His *Portrait of My Mother* (plate 80), done just before her death but enlarged and repainted in 1946, is one of the few other examples. Its quality, largely achieved in the second painting, sprang from recollections made more poignant, perhaps, by his own illness.

"My mother was dying of cancer in a little room on Lexington Avenue. I was sitting talking to her in the window, and I looked at her face and I said, 'Mother, I've never seen anyone with such beautiful eyes.' At that time they had become violet in color instead of brown, the most wonderful pale violet. And she said, 'It's lovely that you say that. It makes me so happy, my son, that you think I have beautiful eyes.' I said, 'Mother, by God, I'd like to paint you.' So she walked over to her little couch-bed, lay down, and crossed her hands over the pain, as she often did, and I got out my paints and went to work. The head and the hands are the result. Much later I enlarged the canvas and added from memory the bony knees and the almost frivolous high-heeled shoes she used to wear. They made a kind of striking contrast to the very spiritual approach to death in her face. I also painted out the banal background I had had before, a bookcase or something, which wasn't adequate to the mystery I wanted in the picture, a kind of moonlike, out-of-the-world quality."

Gradually the shock of Julia's miscarriage and his own operation passed, and

11. SNUG HARBOR. 1942/56.
Oil on canvas, 30 x 25″.
Collection Dr. and Mrs. S. G. Holtzman,
South Fallsburg, New York

Evergood began to return to an active, less introspective life. In 1943 he painted a picture that reveals this change of mood; a portrait of himself grafting an apple tree in the front yard of the little house at Woodside, Queens, where they then lived (plate 12). Not only is the grafting symbolic; everything in the picture strikes a note of gaiety—the bright, clear colors, the unusual degree of realism, and the quasi-primitive simplifications of form, which are a little like Grant Wood's, although Wood could scarcely have drawn so expressive a pair of feet.

Circumstances—America was by now heavily engaged in World War II—and the need to make a living also drew Evergood back into numerous activities. Although he won a purchase prize at the Artists for Victory exhibition at the Metropolitan Museum and sold nine paintings from his third one-man show at the A.C.A. Gallery, he could not yet depend entirely on his art for a livelihood. During the winter of 1942–43 he taught once a week at Muhlenberg College in Allentown, Pennsylvania, and gave private classes in Bethlehem and Philadelphia. In February, 1943, he was invited by the War Department (with ten other artists) to make a pictorial record of the war. He accepted, gave up his teaching jobs, was tentatively assigned to the African front, and went through three busy months of inoculations and equipping. On May 8, however, he and two other artists received identical notes from the Corps of Engineers stating that "it is impossible under existing laws to engage you at this time." Hurrying to Washington to find out the cause of their dismissal, the three were unable to learn the source or the nature of the charges against them. A later letter from the War Department's Bureau of Public Relations (in answer to an appeal which the three had sent to the President) did little to clarify the issue, saying only that an investigation by the Provost Marshal General had developed information that established their employment would be in conflict with provisions of the so-called Hatch Act.

There the matter closed, but something of the bitterness and disappointment Evergood felt erupted in a letter written immediately after the incident: "I love our democratic way of life and have fought for its ideals—freedom of speech—against racial discrimination—and generally for justice and the underdog. It so happened that I saw the menace of Fascism even at the time of the Spanish Civil War —and hated it and said so in my paintings and on the platform. It was natural, therefore, for me to believe that I was being asked to go to a fighting front to record a tremendous human struggle in paint because of the human convictions I had expressed in my life and because of the quality that these convictions had given to my work. . . . It is quite obvious that if there was any cause for my being considered a menace to the national security or the American way of life I would by now be languishing in jail, and should be!"

One of the pictures which Evergood must have had in mind as he wrote was

Fascist Company (plate 55), a canvas symbolic of brutality and destruction, in which he made use, consciously or not, of the inflated nudes and horses conventional in the official art of Hitler and Mussolini. It was soon followed by a number of other paintings on war themes. Some of these dealt with the pathos of human suffering, as in the *Boy from Stalingrad* (plate 62) guarding his mountainous pile of German corpses, an incident related to the artist by the picture's present owner—who had been in Russia during the war—but one which Evergood transformed into a psychological study of youth wrenched prematurely into manhood. More often he attacked war with all the violence he had learned as a social satirist, embellished by a current of imaginative fantasy which began to flow more strongly through all his work at this time. In *The Quarantined Citadel* (plate 13) he banished all the warmongers to an island, equipped them with maps, toy soldiers, and Coney Island airplanes, and let them play out harmlessly their visions of conquest. This picture also marks an interesting though momentary departure from Evergood's usual style; its bristling angularities and forced contrasts of light and dark suggest a German Expressionist influence, particularly that of Beckmann, whose work he had admired in Paris nearly twenty years earlier. Equally fantastic and more characteristic of his own manner are *Renunciation* (plate 81), with its monkeys forswearing man and his atomic weapons, and *New Death* (plate 83), in which a mazelike tree entraps humanity and strews the ground with symbols of destruction.

The war did not, however, have the obsessive quality for Evergood that it had for George Grosz. Throughout the 1940s he continued to paint many other aspects of society. In these works, too, a growing tendency toward fantasy is noticeable, though during the first half of the decade his imagination was held within the bounds of a certain plausibility. *Madonna of the Mines* (plate 66) is the kind of exercise in a fusion of vulgarity and tenderness he had done before, though not with quite such dramatic impact. *A Cup of Tea* and *Still Life* (plates 72, 67) are straight satire; the exaggerations in them are deliberate overstatements for satirical effect. As in the past, he also painted actual incidents, although he often succeeded in endowing them with a symbolic significance that transcended the specific event. One of his best canvases in this vein is *My Forebears Were Pioneers* (plate 14), based on a sight that he saw after the hurricane of 1938.

"We were driving from Cape Cod to New York, going through a little village with all the trees blown down, lying on the lawns, and there was a beautiful, austere old lady—beautiful because she was so ramrod straight—sitting in her chair with an old dog at her feet and a Bible on her knee, calmly looking out at the cars going by, with the complete destruction of her house and trees lying all over the beautiful lawn. I was impressed by the way that old lady of pioneer stock was unperturbed by anything. Her grandfathers had fought Indians and come over on the May-

12. **SELF-PORTRAIT**. 1943.
Oil on canvas, 60 x 36".
Collection Mr. and Mrs. Fred Kraus,
New Rochelle, New York

13. **THE QUARANTINED CITADEL.** 1945.
Oil on canvas, 48 x 39".
Collection
Dr. and Mrs. Leonard Burness,
New York City

flower, and there she was with her Bible, not changed by all that turmoil of nature.

"Julian Levi, the painter, gave the picture its title. He and Bruce Mitchell came into my studio while I was struggling with it, and one of them said, 'It's funny, Phil, how you seem to deal with topical subjects. I don't see things that way.' And I said, 'Well, it is topical now because we've had a hurricane and I saw the old lady sitting there on her lawn, but I don't like to feel that it will always be topical. I don't paint to put over topical ideas. I feel very conscious when I develop a theme that it must have universal connotations before I want to put it down in paint.' "

But as the decade wore on, a new element of pure fantasy, quite unrelated to social or interpretive functions, began to invade even those pictures that ostensibly had social messages. *Moon Maiden* (plate 64) was one of the first. It started as an elaborately symbolic indictment of America's shallower aspects: the nightclub habitués on their tightrope, political prisoners ironically caged in the base of the Statue of Liberty, and Liberty herself remotely situated on the moon. The maiden was intended to be the doll-like woman of the nightclubs, the hatcheck girl, the illusion of pleasure. First he painted her nude, using a model (which he seldom did)—a very beautiful ex-Follies girl with a miraculous body and complexion. In a strange way she increasingly seemed to take over the painting as he worked on it, and when he added the clothes, he found himself molding the skirt into the mysterious cornucopia-like form which dominates the canvas to the virtual obliteration of the social symbolism. Why or whence that shape emerged he could never explain, though by adding the giant hornets he gave it the interpretation of a flower.

An equally inexplicable form encloses the figures in *Men and Mountain* (plate 71)—a gossamer, transparent oval into which the racing skiers have leapt as if into another world where they are frozen forever in their headlong flight. While this picture grew out of an arresting glimpse of ski jumpers near the Bear Mountain Bridge one winter, it has more the look of pure hallucination. It was followed by several paintings, all done in the late 1940s, which are entirely imaginary, totally unrelated to social comment, and in which the fantasy grew wilder than any he had permitted himself before. Thus *Reaching for the Bluebird* (plate 3) confronts a voluptuous nude and a creature that will not be found in any ornithological treatise, both perched high in the branches of a tree. *The Little Captain* (plate 85) serenely rows his skiff through towering waves more improbable than those of Hokusai; it was painted in a single day, Evergood said, for the sheer joy of swirling the paint into that crashing vortex. *Flight of Fancy* (plate 82), like *Kubla Khan,* was an actual dream—one in which the ornate railroad handcar of *The Siding* (plate 45) became the unlikely vehicle for a child borne through the sky by flamingos; when he awoke, the artist hurried to the studio to draw it while the image remained vivid.

50

14. MY FOREBEARS WERE PIONEERS. 1940.
Oil on canvas, 50 x 36".
Georgia Museum of Art,
University of Georgia, Athens

A growing sensuousness, both in the handling of the paint and in the treatment of the female nude, also emerged in Evergood's work during these years. In the 1930s, when he was most deeply involved with social themes, the nude seldom appeared in his work. But from the mid 1940s on, with pictures like *Moon Maiden* and *Reaching for the Bluebird,* it began to play an increasingly important role. Sometimes he treated it as a kind of social symbol. *The Hidden Apple* (plate 77) has that acidulous color and drawing with which he created so vividly the sense of a vital and vulgar humanity; its heroine, with her black panties, skimpy bra, and Ivy League pennants in a drab hall bedroom, tells a story that is not without social significance. But she is also the universal Eve, and her erotic appeal charges the picture with a stronger force than the social message. This is even truer of *Leda in High Places* (plate 88), which started as an elaborate symbol of greed and racial strife, issuing from the rape of the world by a capitalist Zeus, and which ended as one of Evergood's most sensuous nudes, not only in the voluptuous forms with their suggestion of an open, yielding body, but also in the painting itself, the opalescent surface, the melting edges, the feathery brushwork. "Frankly," said Evergood much later, "I don't think the symbolism amounts to a darn."

While Evergood seldom went so far in the direction of pure sensuousness as in *Leda,* he continued to paint many nudes, all of which have a degree of erotic content, though usually tempered by satire or, occasionally, by a kind of tongue-in-cheek outrageousness, a delight in *épatant le bourgeois,* as in his little *Self-Portrait with Nude* (plate 15) with its unmistakable leer. He was always fascinated by the inconsistency of the American attitude toward sex, which bans postcards of Goya's *Maja Desnuda* from the mails but permits the circulation of mail-order catalogues illustrated by demure college girls clad only in their underwear. Something of the absurdity of sex often tinctures his own work, though never to the exclusion of the work's underlying power.

"I think that I was first awakened to the sensuous possibilities of art by my love of Modigliani and Pascin, who were certainly outstanding in their ability to express it. Of course sex was a kind of obsession with Pascin, and I feel that that's a limiting thing. In other words, it's touch and go. It's a little line you walk, a very fine line, and I think that he tends sometimes to go toward a surface sensuality. You might say it's like the difference between a Greek sculptured nude and a bronze Diana with panties on. Tending by nature a little toward the satirical, I think my own work has been more affected by the kind of humor about sex that Goya had sometimes, or Rowlandson and Hogarth. I laugh quite often at the use of it that high-pressure advertising makes in the world today. But I'll be frank: I'm never laughing at the sensuousness of a beautiful woman. I like it. I'm really carried away by the beauty of it, and I want to put some of it down on canvas."

Perhaps the picture which sums up Evergood's attitude most clearly—just as it seems to sum up and bring to fruition every other major tendency in his art up to this point—is *The Jester* (plate 10) of 1950. Here, sensuousness, symbolism, fantasy, humor, satire, and social comment are woven together so inextricably and with such skill that the painting emerges as one of his finest achievements. It is, of course, an allegory of the follies of the world: the glaring mask of war, the little juggler of Wall Street with his fragile eggs, the sinuous, slightly Modigliani-like nudes, the vile brew on the table, presided over by Death, and, beneath the rakish angle of his crown, the recognizable portrait of Evergood himself busily sketching not the scene before him but two poor children with a loaf of bread. Compressed within his characteristically shallow space, the many figures move in an undulating design enlivened by arresting gestures and varied by many countermovements, such as the ladder-like sequence of faces at the right. The brilliant green and red columns and the varicolored harlequin costume of the jester strike the kind of sharp color notes that Evergood likes against the warm pink flesh filling the rest of the picture. The technical mastery and the vivid imagination which has combined such a variety of themes and moods in a unified design of rich complexity is impressive. The picture is an important milestone not only in Evergood's own work, but in the figurative painting of our time.

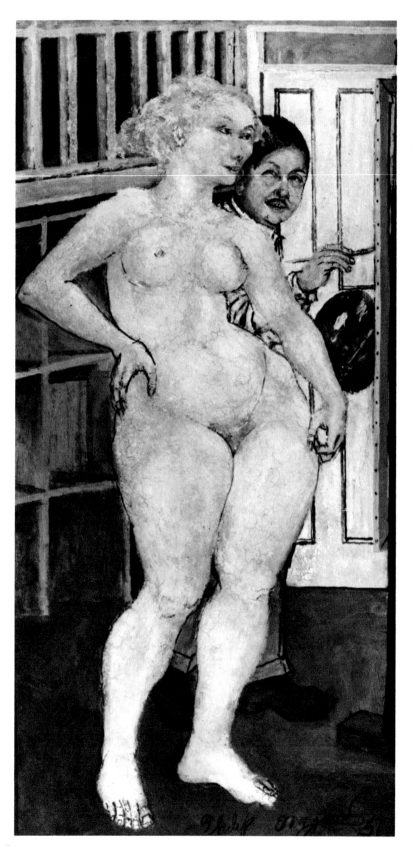

15. SELF-PORTRAIT WITH NUDE. 1951.
Oil on canvas, 31 x 15".
Collection Mr. and Mrs. Bernard Livingston,
New Rochelle, New York

Philip Evergood

REALISM AND FANTASY

Evergood's personal life since the early 1940s was fraught with more of those mercurial changes of fortune which seemed to be his destiny. A low ebb came after his rejection by the Army as an artist-correspondent in 1943. The Federal Art Project was over, he had given up his teaching, and no new opportunities in this field presented themselves. Occasionally his wife found odd jobs as a secretary, but they were not enough to support the family. Impelled by necessity, he found a job with the Midtown Frame Shop, where he was put to mitering and joining the moldings. It was an eight-hour day, the work was tiring, and the pay was not munificent, but it kept them alive. Unfortunately it left him neither the time nor the strength for painting. He was rescued from this impasse by an event which still seems, in retrospect, a near miracle.

"One day I was working away, minding my business, when a little man came in and started ordering some frames. He was giving the measurements to Alex, who ran the shop, and they stood there talking awhile when Alex said, 'Oh, by the way, I didn't introduce you. This is Mr. Joseph Hirshhorn and this is Phil Evergood; he is a painter.' He said, 'I know your work. I've seen it in the Whitney Museum Annuals. I'm rather interested by it. You shouldn't be doing this kind of thing; you should be painting.' Then he went on with his business, but just as he was leaving he came over to the bench and said quietly, 'Would you be interested in bringing some of your canvases to my apartment and showing them to me?' I said, 'Certainly.' He said, 'Well, why don't we make it next Sunday? Get in a taxi, put in as many of your paintings as you can and bring them to my apartment, Number One Fifth Avenue.'

"When I drove up, there was a big commissionaire standing outside in his uniform. Evidently he had been told about my visit, because he paid the taxi and helped me carry my paintings into the elevator, which took me to the top floor. Hirshhorn opened the door of the elevator and helped me out with the pictures himself. He put them all around his beautiful big apartment overlooking the Square, and looked at them, and said, 'Gee, I like that little still life. How much is that?' I said, 'Oh, $150.' He said, 'I'll take it. How much is that other one there?' I said, '$200.' He said, 'How much is that?' It was a larger and better canvas, I thought, so I got more daring and said, '$300.' Well, this went on and by the time he had finished he had bought nine out of the ten or twelve pictures I had taken him and he went over to the desk, sat down and wrote me a big check for the lot. I felt wonderful! He said, 'Now you'll be able to leave the shop. If I were you, I'd get out.' So I finished my month, or whatever it was until they got another man, and left."

The moment was a financial turning point, if not a dramatically decisive one, in Evergood's career. Thereafter he knew poverty and months when the bills could not be paid, but with the help of his wife's earnings he never again faced starvation or was forced to give up his painting for more remunerative work.

After the sale of the nine pictures, the future looked rosier than in many years. He had recovered his strength, his painting was going well, and he was further encouraged when his *Wheels of Victory* (plate 68) won a $2,000 prize in Pepsi-Cola's Portrait of America exhibition in 1944. On a tip from Joseph Hirshhorn, who continued to take a keen interest in his career, he invested the prize money in a certain mining stock, though not without some qualms of conscience when he thought of the savage attacks on Wall Street he had painted at various times and in which, at heart, he still believed. Within six months the value of his investment had risen to $9,000, and he sold out with a mixed sense of guilt and relief. Suddenly they had money. Both he and his wife disliked the suburban atmosphere of Queens; both had longed for a home of their own in the city. They began to comb Greenwich Village, and at 132 Bank Street, near the river, they found a 150-year-old house, dilapidated but beautiful. With the help of a mortgage, they bought and remodeled it, papered and painted the interior, installed an oil furnace in the cellar, raised the roof, and put in a skylight, making the top floor into a pleasant studio.

"We were happy. We had a beautiful little gem of a home in New York. We had one floor we could rent out to help pay for the mortgage. We had even bought a little shack for $1,000 out in Patchogue, Long Island, in the middle of some woods, where we were going to spend the summers. Summer came, so we locked up the Bank Street house and took our two dogs in an old station wagon and went out to Patchogue to be happy. We were all set for life.

"We had a lovely time for six weeks. We had just packed up, ready to come home the next day, and had gone to bed when we heard police sirens in the dead of night in this lonely place. A police car drove up with flooding headlights. I jumped up and rushed downstairs. I didn't know what had happened. The police said, 'Are you Mr. Evergood?' I said, 'Yes.' They said, 'Something terrible has happened. We've been trying all over the place to find you. Your house in New York has been burglarized; someone's been killed. You have to go in immediately, right now, to your house.'

"It was three-thirty in the morning when we arrived at our beautiful little home on Bank Street. All the lights were blazing, every window was smashed, the front door was in the street, ripped off its hinges. We were met on the doorstep by three men in plain clothes. They said, 'You're Mr. Evergood, are you? Well, a terrible thing has happened.' A man, a Negro, had been living in our house for four weeks. A neighbor had seen him going in and out of the basement late at night, but thought possibly he was a friend of mine. Then she noticed there were no lights in the house, except once or twice a candle burning in the studio. So she reported it to the police and they sent a patrol car around. A very famous policeman, who had won many medals for bravery, and a young rookie cop drove up. The older man took out his pistol and cocked it, and they went in the basement with a flashlight. No light was on. When they got to the top floor, to my studio, there was the loud report of a shotgun shell exploding.

"The Negro boy—his name was Gray I discovered later—had taken an old Very pistol, used to shoot flares at sea, which an officer friend had given me. I had hung the darned thing up on the wall just as a bit of decoration, because it was brass and looked cute. He had found a box of shotgun shells that I had in the house and had wound them with tape to make them fit the larger breach of the pistol. He had even practiced with it on the Coney Island shore late at night. It worked. So he shot the policeman in the chest, and tore the whole of his chest away. The young rookie cop—his first time out, mind you—jumped into my little bathroom and shot it out with the Negro boy and wounded him and captured him and took him to jail. By that time the whole place was filled with firemen, policemen, and when they're excited about a thing like that, especially the murder of a policeman, they go to town on everything—tear your curtains down, throw bookcases over, search the place to find out whether there are any clues. The whole house was a shambles, and this great pool of blood in my studio.

"When I got there, they said, 'So you're Mr. Evergood, are you? Well, you're under arrest, my boy.' For having a dangerous weapon—Sullivan Law. They knew as well as I that a Very pistol was not a weapon used normally to kill a man. But it had killed, so I was arrested. I was taken around to the Sixth Precinct station two or three blocks away, and the desk sergeant showed me the Very pistol and said, 'Is that yours?' I said, 'Yes.' He said, 'Well, it's killed the man. That's what killed our great officer. You're a fine kind of a guy to have a weapon around like this, that could kill a man.' I was fingerprinted and about five in the morning they took me down to the Tombs, and I had to walk on a stage like a criminal, where all the detectives were sitting in a darkened auditorium to look at you. They asked me questions about the whole thing, and I told them what I knew. The boy had said I was a friend of his. I refuted that, of course. I had never seen him, never heard of him, knew nothing about him at all, although much later I learned of a mysterious thing that tied him up to me, or rather to my life.

"Anyway, they put me through all the procedures of a regular criminal and threw me into a cell with young hooligans who had been shooting up people, and those boys treated me grand, as if I was one of them now. One young gangster said to me, 'Whatcha in here for?' I said, 'Sullivan Law.' So he said, 'Gee, they'll make it hard for you. You'll get it, boy. You'll get it in the neck. Probably five years they'll send you up for.'"

The months that followed were a nightmare. The painter Frank Kleinholz, who had once been a lawyer, saw Evergood through the indictment and got him released in his own custody pending trial. The first trial, before a one-judge court, failed to reach a verdict. The second trial, before three judges, was more prolonged. At the insistence of Kleinholz and with the help of Hudson Walker and other friends, he engaged one of the country's ablest criminal lawyers, Murray I. Gurfein. Firearms experts were hired who testified that Very pistols had never, to their knowledge, been used as lethal weapons, that they were standard equipment on many small craft, that they could be bought at any marine supply store. An assistant from the lawyer's office was sent to comb antique stores, where he picked up half a dozen old ones that were for sale as ornaments. In the end, two of the three judges voted for acquittal and he was freed. But then he had to be star witness at the murder trial of Gray.

"By the time I got through with that, I never wanted to paint again, I felt my heart was giving out, got into bed, and wouldn't see anybody. I felt terrible, particularly because it was a Negro boy. I *had* to testify against him, and he was electrocuted for the job. It was very strange. He said that he knew me. We found books, scrapbooks, all over the house that he had written in, saying things like 'Phil—Phil Evergood. The great, great painter. Phil Evergood, I have found a toy. I would like to kill with a toy, kill Phil Evergood.' He was waiting for me! My God, he was waiting there to kill me! Probably crazy. And imagine this horror. Julie had been in our house two weeks before the murder. She and a girl friend had spent the night in the bedroom underneath the studio where he was. They thought they

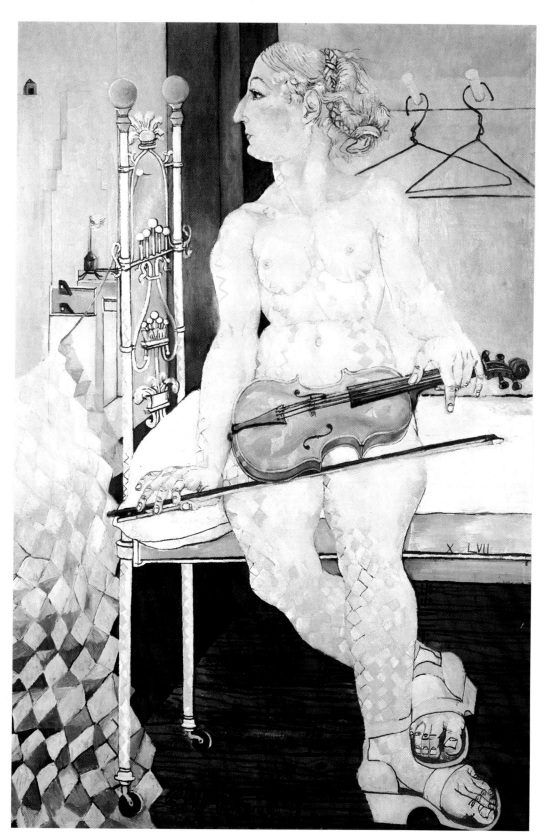

16. NUDE WITH VIOLIN. 1957.
Oil on canvas, 50 x 30″.
Collection Jack Noble,
Roslyn, New York

heard strange noises and were afraid to investigate, so they got up early the next morning and left. And suppose I had arrived there before the police? I'd have been killed, like the cop. So far as my little skin was concerned, I was certainly very lucky.

"Just one other thing about this whole incident. About the time of the trial, I received a letter from another convict on Rikers Island, who told me that he had seen a picture of prisoners I had painted (they were actually political prisoners, not criminals) and that he admired my work tremendously. He sent me a poem he had written to my work (really quite a capable one) and asked me for money, so I sent him a little. I didn't know then that he was connected at all to the boy Gray. But when he got out of prison himself, this other fellow, who was also a Negro youth, he came to see me. I happened to be in the studio, trying to recover my equilibrium, and I was looking for a little teaching job. A beautiful red-haired girl was visiting me at that moment to ask about taking lessons. Here she was, nineteen years old, all excited about the idea, showing me her drawings, telling me exactly when she would start, and 'Oh, it's wonderful, Mr. Evergood,' and I was going to be paid $1.50 an hour and was happy myself because she was attractive and I didn't have to teach someone I didn't like. Suddenly there was a rap on my studio door and in comes a six-foot-two giant with shoulders on him like a prize-fighter. He said, 'Excuse me for barging in like this, but I'm the convict that's been writing you letters.' So I said, 'Stay there a minute. Sit down, will you, I didn't invite you and I'm having a conversation with this lady.' She said, 'Oh dear, well, I must be going, Mr. Evergood, I'll see you tomorrow.' Boom! Out she went. No lessons, no beautiful girl. I never saw her again.

"I turned to the man and said, 'Come into the front room. Sit down. I don't like this intrusion of yours. What do you want?' Well, he told me a long hard-luck story of how he'd been falsely accused of theft, and then had been forced to peddle dope, and had beat up a guy who was running away with his girl friend, and they'd given him a long term, but now he wanted to go straight and could I help him to get a job. Later I did, through a Negro, Judge Silver, whom I'd met recently and whose wife was doing philanthropic work in Harlem. But the point of the story is that he told me about the boy, Gray. He said, 'I met Gray on the Island. Our prison librarian used to be the librarian at Richmond Hill where you painted the mural. He'd show us your pictures and tell us what a wonderful fellow you were. So when Gray got out—he had nowhere to go—he came to visit you. You weren't in so he climbed over a wall and went up your back fire escape and got in. We thought you were a decent guy and wouldn't have minded. I can see you're not as nice as I thought you were.' So there you are. That's the story. That's how the whole thing started."

Evergood was close to nervous collapse by the time these tribulations were over, and even the success of his large retrospective exhibition at the A.C.A. Gallery in 1946 failed to restore his peace of mind. His doctor told him it was imperative for him to leave the city and live in the country if he wished to regain his health. So he sold the Bank Street house, which he had come to hate, and moved out to Patchogue, where he remodeled the shack, adding a concrete studio, and preparing it for year-round living. There his health gradually improved, but it was not a happy solution in the long run. The damp sea air disagreed with his wife, who found it impossible to live there. Alone much of the time, disgusted with the world and himself, he felt trapped in the restless circle of his own unhappiness. He longed to move, but all his funds were tied up in the cottage, which he soon discovered was not easy to sell. With a kind of hopeless desperation he embarked, early in 1952, on a project no artist in his right mind would have undertaken: he decided to paint a prize-winning picture for a museum he had never heard of before, the Terry Art Institute in Miami, which had just announced a nationwide contest. Seating himself at his easel, he put down on canvas the vivid memory of Julia coming through the door with her bags for a weekend, her body alive with the dancer's quick grace. He boxed it himself, sent it off with a prayer, and waited.

It was once again the moment for fortune's wheel to turn. In February it brought him a cryptic notice from the Institute requesting him to appear at Idlewild airport on a certain day and at a certain hour. Arriving, he found a throng of other artists assembled at one of the gates. All of them had paintings in the same exhibition; all had received similar notices. A big chartered plane touched down on the runway. Evergood, with one or two others, was called from the crowd and instructed to climb the landing ramp. When he reached the top, the plane door opened and Mr. Terry emerged, with a check in one hand, and the other outstretched to congratulate him. His picture, *Happy Entrance* (plate 96), had won first purchase prize of $5,000. After brief festivities and the presentation of lesser awards, Mr. Terry remounted his plane and was borne back to Miami, leaving a somewhat dazed group of painters behind him.

The windfall gave Evergood new courage. Nailing a "For Sale" sign to the door, he locked up the cottage at Patchogue and drove to Connecticut, with no very clear idea of where he was going but heading in general for high land away from the water and for the less settled sections where houses were cheap. After some searching he found an old cow barn near Southbury which had already been remodeled as a home by its owner. Using the prize money as a down payment, he bought it in May. He and his wife lived there, and at their nearby home in Bridgewater, Connecticut, until his death.

17. STRANGE BIRD CONTEMPLATING THE DOOM OF MAN. 1960.
Oil on canvas, 30 x 38″. Kennedy Galleries, Inc., New York City

THE LATER SYMBOLISM

In Evergood's painting of the 1950s, a change of atmosphere is apparent—a certain mellowness, a new maturity. On the whole he dealt less often and less bitterly with social problems; the black-and-white moral values and violence of feeling in such earlier works as *American Tragedy* (plate 47) began yielding to symbolism or to satire tempered by detachment—even, perhaps, by a certain indulgence for human weakness. Several of his social paintings of those years did not spring from topical issues at all, but are older canvases which he resurrected and repainted. *The Future Belongs to Them, Toiling Hands* (plates 18, 125), and *The Passing Show* were all first done in the 1930s; all emerged more lyrical in feeling, richer and more subtle in surface, after their repainting in the fifties. Perhaps the most striking transformation of an earlier work is *The New Lazarus* (plate 105), a canvas of 1927 which the artist enlarged around 1940 and reworked at intervals over the succeeding years until it was finished in 1954. During the process, a simple Biblical subject grew gradually into a complex and moving expression of the artist's faith in humanity, a symbolic painting of exceptional sweep and power. The symbols are harsh and direct: racial hatred embodied in the lynched Negro and mourning women; man's cruelty to man in the flayed lamb and figure of Christ (inspired by Grünewald's *Crucifixion*); war in the dead and suffering soldiers; indifference in the hear-nothing, say-nothing, see-nothing figures at the

18. THE FUTURE
BELONGS TO THEM. c. 1938/53.
Oil on canvas, 60 x 40″.
Collection Terry Dintenfass,
New York City

upper right; while out of the tragic panorama Lazarus rises, miraculously, the new man of courage dedicated to truth and to love. In its resonant color, dominated by intense reds and blues, and its extraordinary design, which spins the figures like a whirlwind around the off-center figure of Christ, it is one of Evergood's major achievements in paint and a summation of his whole philosophy of life.

Evergood also turned to new social themes in the 1950s, but he generally treated them with a subtlety and a lightness of touch in considerable contrast to his earlier bludgeoning. *Satisfaction in New Jersey* (plate 94) is a probing psychological study of a self-indulgent mother and her spoiled children; the satirical intent flashes out in the three pairs of blankly staring eyes and the lady's prettily bared teeth. *Woman of Iowa* (plate 19) is a different type, as hard and insensitive as the standardized "ranch" houses behind her, but not without a certain heroic quality, too. The painting in both pictures is perfectly adjusted to their respective moods, soft and feathery in the first, hard as iron in the second. In other canvases the satire dances with a kind of malicious gaiety. *Threshold to Success* (plate 122), which started as a demonstration before a summer class at Duluth University, is a witty projection of the erotic dreams of a young athlete turned scholar. *Enigma of the Collective American Soul* (plate 20) combines in a most unlikely group Eisenhower, Churchill, a beauty-contest winner, and a couple of magazine-cover types; typically Evergoodian are the two urchins stealing a smoke in the corner. There is little moral indignation to be found in any of these canvases, although they betray a remarkably keen eye for American types and American foibles.

But on the whole, Evergood's interest in satire and social comment seems to have waned as he grew older. He was drawn instead toward subjects that he could invest with fantasy or with sensuousness, often both. Perhaps the fantasy is a little more restrained than it was—at least there are fewer dreams and obsessive shapes. But in recompense there is a more pervasive play of the imagination, which manifests itself in that strangeness of eye, that unique way of seeing, which is so indefinable a quality in Evergood's work. It is everywhere: in the unexpectedness of gesture, the intensity of facial expressions, the dislocations of perspective, scale, and proportion; in the texture, the drawing, the color, the shape of everything. The true fantasy in *Juggler of Doom* (plate 127) is not so much the odd contents of the symbolic eggs—an alligator, a snake, a rose, an unborn child, three cherries, gold coins, and a hand grenade—as it is the deadness of the ivory flesh against the red curtains, the almost feminine, wasp-waisted anatomy, the veiled eyes, and the ritualistic gesture. *Woman of Iowa* (plate 19) may be social comment on a recognizable American type, yet what other artist would have conceived the iron brassiere, the blank stare, and the startling prominence of the ribs? There is scarcely a picture in Evergood's later work that does not have, to some degree, that "little

19. WOMAN OF IOWA. 1958.
Oil on canvas, 35 x 30″.
Collection Mr. and Mrs.
George J. Perutz, Dallas

20. **ENIGMA OF THE COLLECTIVE AMERICAN SOUL**. 1959.
Oil on canvas, 70 x 36″.
Collection
Joseph and Mildred Gosman,
Toledo, Ohio

sense of mystery" he so often mentioned, that seeing of things with a kind of wild surprise, as if they had never been seen before, as if they had never been felt before in quite this way. It is the truly fantastic quality in his art, and it deepened steadily throughout his career.

Of course, other and more obvious miracles occurred from time to time. *Artist's Fantasy* (plate 123), with its strange gathering on the grass, its prancing steeds and airborne muse, evokes a lyrical and enigmatic mood, but the essential elements of the picture were established when he first painted it in 1932. The miracles that occur in his later art are more likely to be ones of profusion, for there is something in Evergood which takes a special joy in richness and physical vitality. *The Garden of Betty Mae* (plate 21) engulfs her in its riotous growth, the tiny figure of *Surprised Wader* is nearly lost in the jungle of branches. Sometimes his figures are as lush as the vegetation. The *Farmer's Daughter* and the *American Shrimp Girl* (plates 102, 101) nearly burst their clothes with animal vigor, and both are surrounded by magnificent harvests of sea and land. They are testimony to the artist's undimmed delight in the language of the senses.

In all of Evergood's work of the fifties there is apparent a growing technical mastery and a greater interest in the unlimited possibilities of the painter's craft. His color ranges from the deep, discordant chords of *The New Lazarus* (plate 105) to the pale, singing tones of *David Playing to King Saul* (plate 22), a picture in which the light blues and violets and the brighter yellows and reds seem to echo the very tinkling of the harp. In this, as in many other canvases, the color is instinctively related to the subject with a sureness which grew over the years.

"It is an arbitrary choice, so far as I am concerned. It's not a matter of looking at a piece of nature, like a beautiful field, and selecting the little bits of beautiful color that will interpret it. It's done, with me, by closing my eyes and knowing the color, feeling the color in my brain that I want to use—the nasty color or sickly color, the sweet color, or violent color, or pretty-pretty-dolly color that will express the mood of what I'm trying to put over. I'm not a calculating painter, and it's not an analytical process. It's just a driving instinct at the moment for that piece of nasty green on a tablecloth, we'll say, and a vile, clashing red on a boy's sweater."

If Evergood used color primarily as an expressive tool, he was also fascinated with it for its own sake, and several late canvases seem to be principally concerned with color experiments. In *Nude with Violin* (plate 16), for instance, he plays with the reflections from a brightly checkered curtain on the flesh of the figure. Out of this grew further researches on a similar problem in *Vase and Flowers* (plate 132). Both of these pictures are more purely aesthetic in intent than was Evergood's wont in earlier years, and this is true not only in the matter of color. *Nude with Violin* is also an essay in adapting a Renaissance motif (here, the profile portrait)

21. THE GARDEN OF BETTY MAE. 1958.
Oil on canvas, 40½ x 25½".
Collection Alfredo Valente,
New York City

22. DAVID PLAYING TO KING SAUL. Oil on canvas, 36¾ x 61¼".
Collection Martin Michel, New York City

23. **SAMSON AND THE LION.** 1959.
Oil on wood, 35⅛ x 25″.
Hirshhorn Museum
and Sculpture Garden,
Smithsonian Institution,
Washington, D.C.

to a modern subject—an approach Evergood had tried before in *Leda in High Places* (plate 88), which was frankly inspired by the *Leda* attributed to Leonardo in the Borghese Gallery. These half-playful tributes to past art, in the tradition of the French *hommage* paintings, are further evidence of the artist's concern with the whole range of his traditions.

Evergood was quite conscious, too, of the conflicting poles of tradition in Western art, which are broadly expressed by the terms classicism and romanticism. He was so much the romantic artist himself that his allegiance was naturally with the latter, but at the same time he was always attracted by the clarity and explicitness of statement which are inherent in the classical approach. This attraction produced, throughout his career, a kind of stylistic battle within his own work, a constant tension between the linear and the painterly. The extremes may be seen in the almost completely painterly style of *Samson and the Lion* (plate 23), the almost completely linear handling of *Woman at Piano* (plate 117). Their fusion will be found in almost all his other work, but perhaps most evenly balanced in *Enigma of the Collective American Soul* with its richly shimmering surface accented by sudden passages of forceful drawing.

"I have always alternated to some extent in my painting. After I have cut loose and slashed in and painted with bravura in a certain period of my life, it has then seemed necessary to me that I should teach myself how to paint a beautiful little face with meticulousness and control. That was what my general progress needed. I have always been conscious of trying not to go too far in one direction, because if I did, I knew that I would either become an academician or perhaps a Pollock type of painter, and I didn't want to be either. I wanted to be as free and as daring as a Pollock, and I wanted to be as disciplined as a Giotto—if I could.

"Of course subject has something to do with it. *Samson and the Lion*, for instance, has practically nothing linear about it; it's just the paint laid on with a trowel. The violence of the theme seemed to call for the violent handling of the paint, in a kind of fierce explosion of slashing. Whereas another painting, like the *Boy from Stalingrad* [plate 62] perhaps, is small in scale and needs a great deal of precious little detail to bring out his youth and the little sorrow in his face. Sometimes just the scale of the canvas itself determines how you paint.

"But beyond these considerations I do believe that the whole interest of art depends very much on the relationship of sharpness to softness, of disappearing edge to defined edge, on the lack of monotony between the accented moment and the let-go moment. You don't always feel strong enough to do that. I've done drawings that I've looked at afterwards and found banal and monotonous because I hadn't been inspired at the time to know where to accent one sweeping line with another brittle, wiry line. But on the other hand, when I feel that I've been successful—especially in my paintings—it's always been the little sharp drawing of a toe or a finger or an eyelid in relation to a big kind of smoothness and lost-edge quality that has made it any good at all."

The extraordinary versatility of Evergood's draftsmanship appears most clearly, perhaps, in a series of big drawings he did in 1954–55. In these his line varies widely. It can be emphatic and deliberately awkward, as it is in *Put to Pasture* (plate 24), where every rivet of the old locomotive and every stripe in the engineer's coat is drawn with an insistence which might be monotonous were it not for the character and variety of the strokes. It can also be as subtle and precise as a sharp-focus photograph and much more incisive in rendering character, as it is in *Dear Aunt Susie* (plate 25). It can be bold and summary, suggesting a whole range of forms and textures with a minimum of means, as it is in *Man Reading* (plate 107). It can bound with a wild humor of its own, quite disregarding natural shapes and proportions, as it does in *Lolly with Her Hair Down* (plate 114). And it can perform the most delicate and sinuous of arabesques, as it does in the floating tresses of *Julia* (plate 113).

A greater linear virtuosity is also apparent in some of the later paintings. Early in his career Evergood discovered the extraordinary expressiveness of child art and developed from it a bold, direct drawing of his own, marked by a certain conscious naiveté of handling. He uses it again in pictures like *Resort Beach*, *Threshold to Success,* or *Girl and Sunflowers* (plates 116, 122, 91), although it has come to look less like its source and more like pure Evergood. But this is only one facet in a more complex style. As he grew older, Evergood permitted a natural decorative sensibility to develop more freely in essentially flat patterns of great variety and beauty. *Woman at Piano* (plate 117) is one of the most striking examples, a picture organized in very shallow space with a remarkably sensitive relation between the silhouetted shapes and, above all, a superb play of line as it ranges from the flowing curves of the figure and the piano through the wiry foliage, the staccato marks of the music, and on to the stark bars of window, music rack, and floor. The same decorative sense invades many other later pictures. It can be seen in the richly patterned background of *American Shrimp Girl* and her own robust silhouette, in the Victorian bedstead and the black wire coat hangers which add so much visually to *Nude with Violin* (plate 16), or in the vibrant web of branches which enclose *Surprised Wader.*

In retrospect, its beginnings can be perceived in a few earlier pictures, such as *Nude by the El* or *Juju as a Wave* (plates 5, 60), but it was only in the fifties that it emerged fully as a major element in his work.

This emergence was a part of Evergood's maturity as an artist. It was closely linked with the wider problem of design, which came to absorb him more and more

24. **PUT TO PASTURE**. 1954.
Brush and ink, gouache,
and charcoal, 37¾ x 25″.
Hirshhorn Museum
and Sculpture Garden,
Smithsonian Institution,
Washington, D.C.

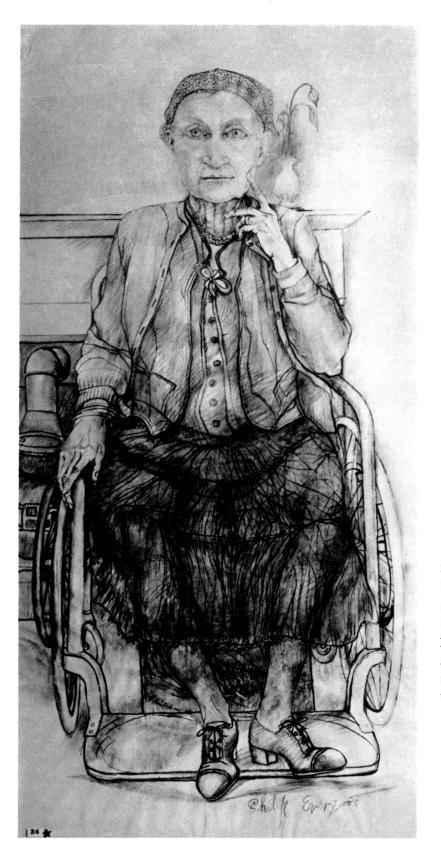

25. **DEAR AUNT SUSIE**. 1954.
Brush and ink, pencil,
gouache, chalk, and
charcoal, 44¾ x 22⅝".
Hirshhorn Museum
and Sculpture Garden,
Smithsonian Institution,
Washington, D.C.

with the passage of years. Early in the 1930s he had established a preference for closely knit compositions, strongly related to the picture plane, but in the urgency of his concern with other matters—with social problems, with fantasy, and with the whole development of a personal style—he had tended to organize his pictures either quite simply, as in single figures like *Lily and the Sparrows,* or as turbulent waves of action, a little casual in their formal relations, as in *Street Corner.* There were, of course, exceptions. The Richmond Hill murals were designed with a great deal of thought and skill, and a few pictures, like *The Pink Dismissal Slip,* were more subtly built. After the early 1940s, Evergood worked with increasing sensibility on consciously wrought designs which, though still contained for the most part within the shallow space he preferred, have both a stronger and a less obvious architecture. His most powerful and his most complex compositions, already discussed, came only in the 1950s, with *The Jester* and *The New Lazarus* (plates 10,105).

"I have often thought that all good artists develop a better sense of design as they grow older. Design is the hardest thing we do. Solving its problems comes later—it comes last. Think of the great Titians of his old age. Or compare the early Giottos with the late ones. The early pictures don't have that odd balance, that holding together with great strength yet pulling away from balance that you find in the late work, which has the terrific structure of a great piece of architecture that will never collapse but is never monotonous or symmetrical.

"In my own work I sometimes sit down with a canvas and divide it up—draw a diagonal, as some of the old masters did, and fit little shapes and things around it the way an abstract painter would—a Mondrian type of abstract painter. Then I begin to paint the thing I want to paint within those little areas. Afterwards I take a great deal of liberty in covering the structure up so it won't be too obvious—not that I want to hide my method but because it seems more intriguing that way. Sometimes, of course, the urge strikes me to just abandon all reason and get to work slashing in the design, not even caring how the work goes on the canvas. But lots of my paintings have been worked the first way, though they may not look it."

In 1960 the Whitney Museum of American Art gave Evergood a large retrospective exhibition, arranged by the writer. Predictably, the critical reactions were strong; no one has ever been lukewarm about Evergood's work. "I see mostly secondhand Chagall and Beckmann, much compositional confusion and a great deal of ugly crudity," wrote Alfred Frankenstein in the *San Francisco Chronicle.* "His pictures were and remain so exuberant, so astonishingly alive, so intense that even the teeth and toenails are a proper part of his expression, like little black wires crackling with electricity," said Emily Genauer in *The New York Herald Tribune.*

Isolated from New York in his Connecticut retreat—which he seldom left in his late years—Evergood appears to have been little affected by this mixed reception. He was, after all, used to it. It may have contributed, however, to his loneliness and to a growing sense of alienation from the city, even from American life. This in turn had an appreciable effect on his art during the 1960s, turning him away from topical issues, throwing him back on his own nature, his earlier experiences, his imagination, and his reading—in short, making his late art more introspective in character.

For one thing, there are noticeably fewer paintings dealing with social issues, and those that do seem more remote, even fanciful. *Strange Bird Contemplating the Doom of Man* (plate 17) is an apocalyptic vision, a symbol rather than an event. "I found the bird, a harpie, in an old French book. It's part hawk, part eagle, part vulture, part owl. But its feathers were pretty colors in the book so I used them in the painting." One of the few other socially oriented canvases of the sixties is *Minehead: In Memory of Zola's Germinal* (plate 148), of literary inspiration as its title suggests.

Also literary in inception are *Circus* (plate 147), which Evergood painted after reading a biography of Toulouse-Lautrec which awoke memories of the Fratellini brothers and the Cirque Medrano. Similarly, *Don Quixote and the Windmill* (plate 26) grew out of a rereading of Cervantes. "I thought of all the illustrations done of Don Quixote and none seemed plastic enough, so I thought I would just cut loose and do him in a rather abstract and Expressionistic way." It is important to distinguish, in these cases, between literary inspiration and literary treatment. Evergood never converted the one into the other. He simply used his reading as a spur to his imagination, which often carried him far from his sources. Certainly *Don Quixote,* like his earlier *Samson and the Lion* (plate 23), is one of his most vigorous essays in Expressionism; it is in no sense an illustration.

Indeed, Evergood's imagination did not need a literary spur; it embroidered on recollections of childhood, on little events of daily life, on sudden perceptions magnified. *Forest and Riders* (plate 141) grew from a visit to the so-called Cathedral Pines near Kent, Connecticut, and the sight of a single figure leading a horse; multiplied to a sweeping throng, it reflects the leap of the artist's imagination into mystery. Often the event is more prosaic. The cat knocks over a wineglass and bowl of fruit, their dog filches a steak from the dining room table, and we have the wild strident humor of *Big Peter and the Oranges* (plate 143) and *Dog at Table* (plate 27). In several instances Evergood's pictures grew from a combination of chance encounter, imagination, and purely aesthetic considerations. An example is *Taming the Tiger* (plate 29). "When we moved into this house [in Bridgewater], up in the attic was a great big tiger rug with a stuffed head, showing teeth. I thought

26. DON QUIXOTE AND THE WINDMILL.
1964. Oil on canvas, 36 x 31″.
Collection Dr. and Mrs.
Arthur E. Kahn, New York City

27. DOG AT TABLE. 1966.
Oil on canvas, 27 x 19⅜".
Kennedy Galleries, Inc.,
New York City

the head would make a good still life, so to speak, interesting forms, so I began studying the head and the painting came out of that. So then I thought, where would this tiger be? Out in the jungles of India, and how interesting to put the white flesh of a woman next to all those stripes as a foil to the rather dullness of just the tiger."

Recollections of the past were also the starting point of several pictures. *Swimming Lesson* (plate 139) was "probably a memory of my youth when my father used to put me on his back and wade right in, scaring me to death. The geese flying over are just to make the scene a little weird or mysterious." *Tea for Two* (plate 138) reconstructs a vaguely remembered scene. "An old lecherous man with a young little dilly of a girl—a pretty little darling—he in cutaway and striped trousers, sits there giving her a lot of attention to ingratiate himself with her."

But perhaps Evergood's strongest works of the sixties are his nudes. A series of canvases—*Look Homeward Marilyn, The Ancient Queen, Pristine Bather, Nude with Little Dog* (plates 30, 129, 140, 144)—reiterates the sensuous pleasure he had always taken in painting the female body. The sly humor which tempered the sensuousness of his earlier nudes yields in these pictures to a more poignant expression. They reflect an older man's awareness of the poetry and mystery of sex, not untinged with sadness. It is perhaps no accident that two of the four pictures deal with women taking their own lives. *The Ancient Queen* is plainly Cleopatra. Of his tribute to Marilyn Monroe he says only: "She looked homeward too late. She'd taken her pills, staggered to the phone. But she looked homeward too late."

Another strand in Evergood's art of the sixties is the occasional exercise of his great gift for decorative calligraphy—sometimes in drawings like *Lady in Brocade Chemise* (plate 145), sometimes in the more massive rhythms of oils like *Still Life with Candy Stick Vase* or *Still Life with Hornets and Crocuses* (plates 31, 151). If these lack some of the exuberance of his earlier floral extravaganzas, they have gained in solidity and powerfully orchestrated structure.

In about 1963, Evergood moved to a beautiful eighteenth-century farmhouse just outside Bridgewater, Connecticut. Three years later he fell on the stairs and was hospitalized with a concussion. He recovered and began to paint again. Then, only a year later, the flying head of a match he was striking set fire to a highly flammable shirt and in seconds he was enveloped in flame. Again he was hospitalized, this time for weeks as his severe burns were treated with silver nitrate. He thereafter painted no major works.

But the record of his accomplishment is ample, for he had over forty years of a prolific career behind him at his death in 1973. And if one impression emerges more clearly than any other in considering his work as a whole during his long span, it is perhaps the consistency with which it has mirrored his character and his

28. LADY WITH FRUIT. 1948.
Oil on canvas, 35 x 23″.
Collection Dr. and
Mrs. Robert E.
Rothenberg, New York

29. **TAMING THE TIGER.** 1967. Oil on canvas, 30 x 40″.
Kennedy Galleries, Inc., New York City

30. LOOK HOMEWARD MARILYN. 1963.
Oil on canvas, 46 x 36".
Collection Mr. and Mrs. Joseph James Akston,
Palm Beach, Florida

31. STILL LIFE WITH CANDY STICK VASE. 1967. Oil on canvas, 20 x 16".
Collection Mr. and Mrs. Herbert A. Goldstone, New York City

32. NEW ENGLAND LANDSCAPE. 1940. Oil on canvas, 37 x 39".
The Harry N. Abrams Family Collection, New York City

preoccupations and the events of his life. This is no accident. Evergood consciously willed it so, and was often wounded in consequence, for he kept his sensibilities almost totally unprotected. He had to weep or laugh in life with the same intensity that he wept or laughed on canvas. And he had to translate the emotions of life into the very different language of art with the utmost immediacy of feeling. In this he was a hard and self-critical perfectionist who, like Ryder, hated to part with a canvas and would repaint it many times over long periods unless forcibly prevented. (He startled one collector who returned a picture to him for minor repairs by filling the sky with wildly swooping airplanes.) Despite the fact that he painted many hasty and even some downright bad canvases, he never painted a dull or a conventional one.

Perhaps one very small portrait of himself with a divining rod (plate 108), painted about 1954, sums up the story best. Here, symbolized, is the search of the idealist; here, too, are the wild and staring eyes, the sensuous mouth, the unabashed sense of drama in his own being, and, beneath it, the undercurrent of ironic humor. With all his mercurial changes of mood and of style there is, at the core, one essential Evergood—a man touched with madness, not in the clinical sense but in the divine one of the Greeks. Or if this seems too heroic a figure of speech for an artist so deeply concerned with the realities of daily living, let us say in the more modern meaning which Schiller intended when he wrote, in a letter of 1788: "Apparently it is not good—and indeed it hinders the creative work of the mind—if the intellect examines too closely the ideas already pouring in, as it were, at the gates. Regarded in isolation, an idea may be quite insignificant, and venturesome in the extreme, but it may acquire importance from an idea which follows it. . . . In the case of a creative mind, it seems to me, the intellect has withdrawn its watchers from the gates, and the ideas rush in pell-mell, and only then does it review and inspect the multitude. You worthy critics, or whatever you may call yourselves, are ashamed or afraid of the momentary and passing madness which is found in all real creators, the longer or shorter duration of which distinguishes the thinking artist from the dreamer."

Evergood was both.

33. MYTHOLOGY. 1925. Oil on canvas, 21 x 28½".
Collection Mr. and Mrs. Harris J. Klein, Brooklyn, New York

34. CENTAURS AND MEN. 1926-27. Etching, 7 x 9¼"

35. "HE ASKED THE WAVES AND ASKED
THE FELLON WINDS." 1928-29. Etching, 6¼ x 8″

36. DEATH OF ABSALOM. 1930-31.
Etching, engraving, drypoint, 8 x 13¾″

37. VARIATION ON A CLASSICAL THEME, II. c. 1927. Watercolor, 15¼ x 16½".
Collection Mr. and Mrs. John Davies Stamm, Walpole, New Hampshire

38. JACOB WRESTLING WITH THE ANGEL. 1929. Oil on canvas, 12 x 16″.
Collection Alfredo Valente, New York City

39. SOLOMON AT THE COURT OF SHEBA. c. 1929. Oil on canvas, 41 x 48".
Collection Sally Edwoods, Jules and Sheldon Fleitman, New York City

40. DANCE MARATHON. 1934.
Oil on canvas, 60 x 40".
University Art Museum,
University of Texas at Austin.
The Michener Collection

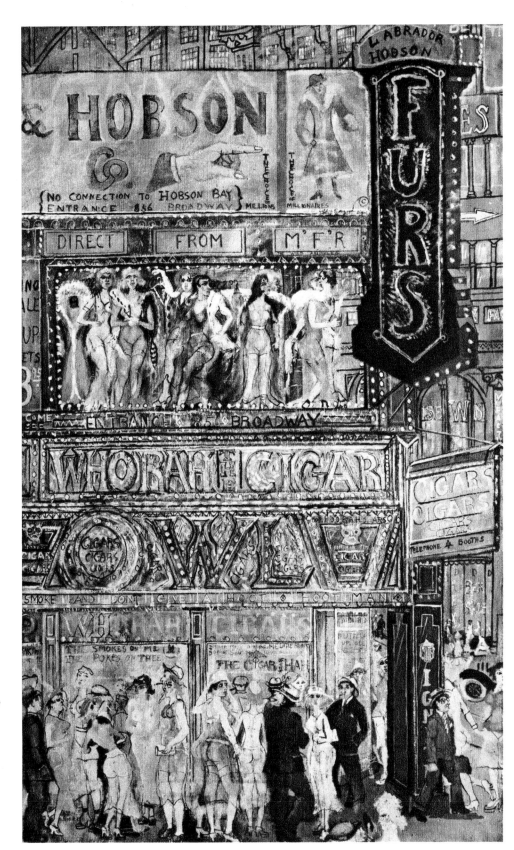

42. TREADMILL. C. 1936.
Oil on canvas, 49 x 29".
Collection Herbert R. Steinmann,
New York City

43. ALL IN A DAY'S WORK. 1936. Oil on canvas, 24 x 40".
Syracuse University Art Collection, Syracuse, New York. Gift of Mr. and Mrs. Harris J. Klein

44. STREET CORNER. 1936.
Oil on canvas, 30 x 55″.
Collection Mr. and Mrs.
Himan Brown, New York City

45. THE SIDING. 1936. Oil on canvas, 36 x 27".
A.C.A. Gallery, New York City

46. SPRING. 1934.
Oil on canvas, 25 x 30". Private collection

47. AMERICAN TRAGEDY. 1936. Oil on canvas, 29½ x 39½".
Collection Mrs. Gerritt Pieter Van de Bovenkamp, New York City

49. MINE DISASTER. 1937. Oil on canvas, 40 x 70″.
Collection Mr. and Mrs. Himan Brown, New York City

50. THE PINK DISMISSAL SLIP. 1937.
Oil on canvas, 28 x 22½".
Herbert F. Johnson Museum of Art,
Cornell University, Ithaca, New York

51. THE STORY OF RICHMOND HILL
(detail of plate 9). 1936-37.
Richmond Hill Library,
New York City

52. **THE STORY OF RICHMOND HILL** (detail of plate 9)

53. THE STORY OF RICHMOND HILL (detail of plate 9)

54. THE STORY OF RICHMOND HILL
(detail of plate 9)

55. FASCIST COMPANY. C. 1942.
Oil on canvas, 44 x 31″.
Collection
Mr. and Mrs. John Davies Stamm,
Walpole, New Hampshire

56. COTTON FROM FIELD TO MILL. 1938. United States Post Office, Jackson, Georgia

57. FAT OF THE LAND. 1941.
Oil on canvas, 28 x 46″.
Museum of Fine Arts, Boston.
Charles Henry Hayden Fund

58. **THE BIG NOISE.** 1941. Oil on canvas, 30 x 35".
Collection Mr. and Mrs. Allan Harvey, Scarsdale, New York

59. KALAMAZOO IN WINTER. 1941-42. Oil on canvas, 30 x 35".
The Metropolitan Museum of Art, New York City. Arthur H. Hearn Fund, 1950

60. JUJU AS A WAVE. 1932-50.
Oil on canvas, 68 7/8 x 43 3/8".
Hirshhorn Museum and Sculpture Garden,
Smithsonian Institution, Washington, D.C.

61. THROUGH THE FOG
(SELF-PORTRAIT). 1942.
Oil on canvas, 22 x 18″.
Private collection

62. BOY FROM STALINGRAD. 1943.
Oil on canvas, 25 x 18".
Collection Mr. and Mrs.
John Davies Stamm,
Walpole, New Hampshire

63. DON'T CRY MOTHER. 1938-44.
Oil on canvas, 26 x 18″.
The Museum of Modern Art,
New York City. Purchase

64. MOON MAIDEN. 1944.
Oil on canvas, 40 x 35″.
Collection Bella and Sol Fishko,
New York City

65. TURMOIL. 1943.
Oil on canvas mounted
on fiberboard, 24¼ x 20⅜".
Hirshhorn Museum
and Sculpture Garden,
Smithsonian Institution,
Washington, D.C.

66. MADONNA OF THE MINES. 1932/44.
Oil on canvas, 48 x 29".
Collection Mr. and Mrs. Howard Weingrow,
Old Westbury, New York

67. STILL LIFE. 1944. Oil on canvas, 34½ x 39½".
Collection Ione and Hudson Walker, Forest Hills, New York

68. WHEELS OF VICTORY. 1944. Oil on canvas, 37 x 41½″. Collection Ione and Hudson Walker,
Forest Hills, New York. On longterm loan to the University Art Gallery, University of Minnesota, Minneapolis

69. NO SALE. 1945.
Oil on canvas, 26 x 21″.
The Baltimore Museum of Art

70. ARTIST IN SOCIETY. 1936.
Oil on plywood, 60 x 36″.
Private collection

71. MEN AND MOUNTAIN. 1945. Oil on canvas, 42 x 48″.
Collection Mr. and Mrs. Harris J. Klein, Brooklyn, New York

72. A CUP OF TEA. 1946.
Oil on canvas, 33 x 25″.
Collection Lily Harmon,
New York City

73. DAWN. 1946. Oil on canvas, 40½ x 19¼″.
Collection Ben Margolin, New York City

74. TWILIGHT LANDSCAPE. 1925/47. Oil on canvas, 24 x 17½″.
Collection Eve Merriam Lewin, New York City

75. GRAND STAND PLAY. 1946. Oil on canvas, 25 x 40″.
Collection Mr. and Mrs. William A. Marsteller, New York City

76. DREAM CATCH. 1946.
Oil on canvas, 30 x 20⅞".
Hirshhorn Museum
and Sculpture Garden,
Smithsonian Institution,
Washington, D.C.

77. THE HIDDEN APPLE. 1946.
Oil on canvas, 40 x 24½".
Collection Mr. and Mrs. Harris J. Klein,
Brooklyn, New York

78. SNOW CITY. 1947.
Oil on canvas, 26 x 32″. Private collection

79. LAUGHING WORKER. 1948.
Oil on canvas (destroyed)

80. PORTRAIT OF MY MOTHER. 1927/46.
Oil on canvas, 36 x 23″.
Museum of Fine Arts,
Foundation for the Arts Collection, Dallas.
Gift of Marvin Small

81. RENUNCIATION. 1946.
Oil on canvas, 50 x 36″.
Collection Mr. and Mrs. Harris J. Klein,
Brooklyn, New York

83. NEW DEATH. 1947.
Oil on canvas, 37 x 31¾".
Collection
Charles Gwathmey, Amagansett,
New York

84. HER WORLD. 1948.
Oil on canvas, 48 x 35⅝″.
The Metropolitan Museum of Art, New York City.
Arthur H. Hearn Fund, 1950

85. THE LITTLE CAPTAIN. 1948.
Oil on canvas, 48½ x 37½".
Neuberger Museum,
State University of New York
at Purchase

87. THE FORGOTTEN MAN. c. 1949.
Oil on canvas, 60 x 40″.
Brandeis University Art Collection,
Waltham, Massachusetts.
Gift of Mr. and Mrs. Harris J. Klein

88. LEDA IN HIGH PLACES. 1949.
Oil on canvas, 45 x 30″.
Collection Terry Dintenfass,
New York City

89. SUNNY SIDE OF THE STREET. 1950.
Oil on canvas, 50 x 36¼".
The Corcoran Gallery of Art,
Washington, D.C.

90. FISHERMEN. 1951.
Oil on canvas, 27 x 18″.
Collection Bella and Sol Fishko,
New York City

91. GIRL AND SUNFLOWERS. 1951.
Oil on canvas, 35 x 26″.
Collection Mr. and Mrs.
Stanley J. Wolf,
Great Neck, New York

92. MOM'S CATHEDRAL. 1951. Oil on canvas, 36 x 46".
Collection L. Arnold Weissberger, New York City

93. PORTRAIT OF AN ARTIST
AS A YOUNG MAN.
c. 1936/48/51.
Oil on canvas, 35 x 25".
Private collection

95. DOWAGER IN A WHEELCHAIR. 1952.
Oil on canvas, 48 x 36″.
The Sara Roby Foundation,
New York City

96. HAPPY ENTRANCE. 1951.
Oil on canvas, 28 x 20".
Collection Dr. and Mrs. David A. Epstein,
Huntington Woods, Michigan

97. PORTRAIT OF THE KLEINHOLZ FAMILY.
1953. Oil on canvas, 43 x 35″.
Collection Frank
and Lidia Kleinholz, Miami

98 NATURE WITHOUT MAN. 1952. Oil on wood, 30 x 19¼".
Hirshhorn Museum and Sculpture Garden,
Smithsonian Institution, Washington, D.C.

99. BLASTERS—MESABI MINE. 1954. Watercolor, 39 x 19½".
Collection Allied Maintenance Corporation,
New York City

100. SEEKING A FUTURE. 1952.
Oil on canvas, 24 x 18".
Collection Mrs. Murray Handwerker,
Lawrence, New York

101. AMERICAN SHRIMP GIRL. 1954.
Oil on canvas
mounted on wood, 46¼ x 32⅜".
Hirshhorn Museum
and Sculpture Garden,
Smithsonian Institution,
Washington, D.C.

102. FARMER'S DAUGHTER. 1954.
Oil on canvas, 30 x 24".
Collection Andrew Dintenfass,
Philadelphia

103. GIRL READING. 1954.
Brush and ink, chalk,
and charcoal, 33½ x 25¼″.
Hirshhorn Museum
and Sculpture Garden,
Smithsonian Institution,
Washington, D.C.

104. THE MCCONNEY FLATS. 1954. Oil on canvas, 14 x 23¾".
Collection Gladys and Selig Burrows, Mill Neck, New York

105. THE NEW LAZARUS. 1927/54. Oil on canvas, 48 x 83¼″.
Whitney Museum of American Art, New York City. Gift of Joseph H. Hirshhorn

106. STRANGE BIRDS. 1954.
Brush and ink, 38 x 25″.
Hirshhorn Museum
and Sculpture Garden,
Smithsonian Institution,
Washington, D.C.

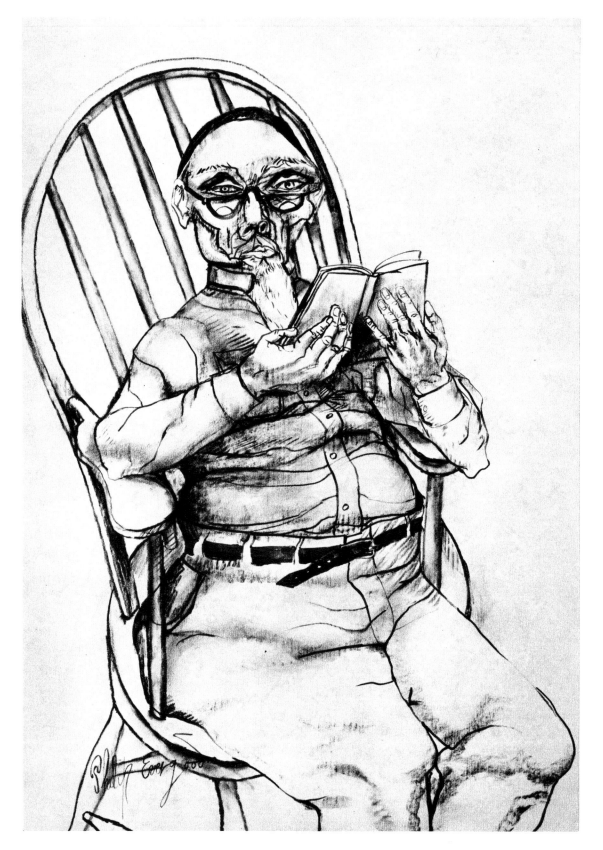

107. MAN READING. 1954.
Brush and ink,
and charcoal, 37½ x 24¾".
Hirshhorn Museum
and Sculpture Garden,
Smithsonian Institution,
Washington, D.C.

108. SELF-PORTRAIT
WITH DIVINING ROD. C. 1954.
Oil on canvas, 15½ x 11½".
Collection Mrs. Gerritt Pieter
Van de Bovenkamp, New York City

109. VALCONIC VASES. 1964.
Oil on canvas, 22 x 15″.
Collection Mr. and Mrs.
Harris J. Klein,
Brooklyn, New York

110. ALONE. 1955.
Oil on canvas, 36 x 25″.
Collection Mr. and Mrs.
Louis Smith, New York City

111. BATHERS. C. 1955.
Oil on canvas, 20 x 15″.
Collection Edmund E. Levin,
New York City

112. EPITAPH. c. 1953-55. Oil on canvas, 55 x 72″.
Kennedy Galleries, Inc., New York City

113. JULIA. 1955.
Brush and ink, 36¾ x 23¼".
Collection Bella and Sol Fishko,
New York City

114. LOLLY WITH HER HAIR DOWN. 1955.
Charcoal and chalk, 37⅝ x 24¾".
Hirshhorn Museum
and Sculpture Garden,
Smithsonian Institution,
Washington, D.C.

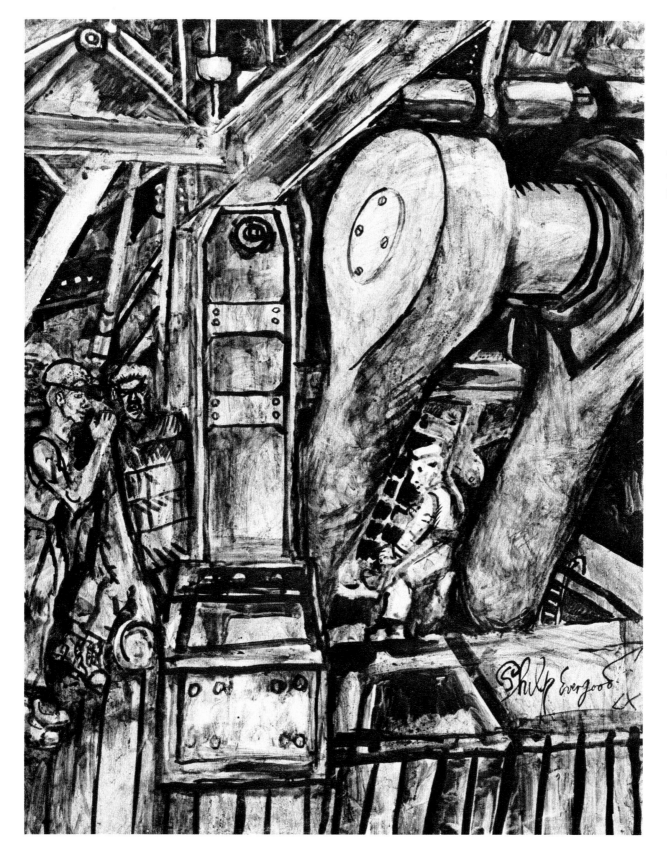

115. THE MACHINE. 1960.
Wash drawing, 23½ x 18″.
Collection Herbert S. Adler,
Scarsdale, New York

116. RESORT BEACH. 1955.
Oil on canvas, 31½ x 21".
Collection Mr. and Mrs. Lewis Garlick,
New York City

117. WOMAN AT PIANO. 1955.
Oil on canvas, 59½ x 35⅜".
National Collection of Fine Arts,
Smithsonian Institution,
Washington, D.C.

118. MUSIC. 1933-56. Oil on canvas, 6 x 10′.
Collection Mr. and Mrs. Harris J. Klein, Brooklyn, New York

119. WATERFRONT. 1935/55. Oil on canvas, 60 x 30″.
Collection Mr. and Mrs. M. Toberoff, New York City

120. ROADBUILDERS. 1956. Oil on canvas, 50 x 36″.
Collection Ella Freidus, New York City

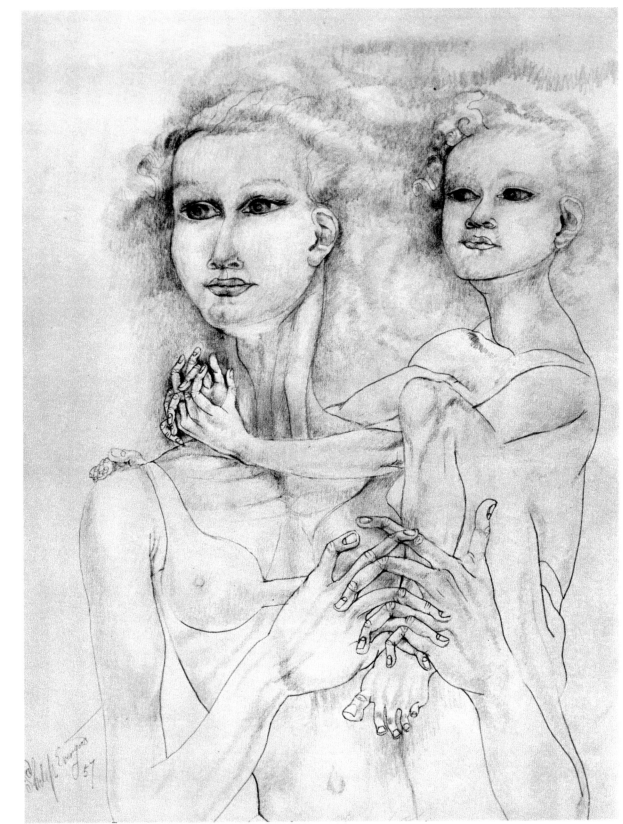

121. MOTHER AND CHILD. 1957.
Pencil, 27⅛ x 18″.
Collection Terry Dintenfass,
New York City

122. THRESHOLD TO SUCCESS. 1955/57.
Oil on panel, 65 x 36″.
The Pennsylvania Academy
of the Fine Arts, Philadelphia

123. ARTIST'S FANTASY. 1932/58.
Oil on canvas, 84 x 48″.
Collection Mrs. Gerritt Pieter
Van de Bovenkamp,
New York City

124. DUSK AT FUJI. 1927/58. Oil on canvas, c. 26 x 32″.
Collection Mr. and Mrs. Russell Morton Brown, Alexandria, Virginia

125. TOILING HANDS. c. 1939/57-58. Oil on canvas, 24 x 30″.
A.C.A. Gallery, New York City

126. JUJU AND HER DOG COPELIA. 1958.
Oil on canvas mounted on wood, 24 x 18″
Hirshhorn Museum
and Sculpture Garden,
Smithsonian Institution,
Washington, D.C.

127. JUGGLER OF DOOM. 1958.
Oil on canvas.
Collection Mr. and Mrs.
Edward L. Neustadter,
Harrison, New York

128. TWO SUSANNAS. c. 1940-59. Oil on canvas, 24 x 48".
Collection Dr. and Mrs. Harvey Amsterdam, Plainview, New York

130. COOL DOLL IN POOL. 1959.
Oil on canvas, 35 x 25″.
Collection David A. Teichman,
New York City

131. SUCCESS TEAM. 1959.
Oil on canvas, 22 x 18".
Collection
Peter Sammartino,
Rutherford, New Jersey

132. VASE AND FLOWERS. 1959.
Oil on canvas, 44 x 30″.
Collection Ella Freidus,
New York City

133. BUTCHER BOY. After 1960.
Oil on copper, 28 x 22″.
Collection
Mr. and Mrs. Allan Harvey,
Scarsdale, New York

134. VIRGINIA IN THE GROTTO. 1959.
Oil on canvas, 50 x 30″.
Whitney Museum of American Art,
New York City.
Living Arts Foundation Fund

135. GIRL AND BLUE ROSE. 1960.
Charcoal and watercolor, 24 x 19".
Collection Ella Freidus,
New York City

136. SUBURBAN TWILIGHT. 1960.
Charcoal, 32 ⅞ x 20″.
Collection Andrew Dintenfass,
Philadelphia

137. ESCAPE. 1961.
Oil on Masonite, 40 x 36″.
Collection Ella Freidus,
New York City

138. TEA FOR TWO. 1927/61.
Oil on canvas, 21¼ x 17¾″.
Collection
Mr. and Mrs. John Davies Stamm,
Walpole, New Hampshire

139. SWIMMING LESSON. 1961.
Oil on canvas, 40 x 30″.
Kennedy Galleries, Inc.,
New York City

140. PRISTINE BATHER. 1963.
Oil on canvas, 39¾ x 29½".
Kennedy Galleries, Inc.,
New York City

141. FOREST AND RIDERS. 1963.
Oil on canvas, 46 x 36".
Kennedy Galleries, Inc.,
New York City

142. DANCER IN PEARL GREYS. 1964.
Oil on canvas, 60 x 38″.
Kennedy Galleries, Inc.,
New York City

143. BIG PETER
AND THE ORANGES. 1964.
Oil on canvas, 36 x 30″.
Kennedy Galleries, Inc.,
New York City

144. NUDE WITH LITTLE DOG. 1964.
Oil on canvas, 64 x 34".
Kennedy Galleries, Inc.,
New York City

145. LADY IN BROCADE
CHEMISE. 1964.
Drawing, 24¼ x 19¼".
Collection Mr. and Mrs.
Joseph James Akston,
Palm Beach, Florida

146. THE PORTUGUESE SHAWL. 1963.
Oil on canvas, 35 x 25″.
Collection
Mr. and Mrs. Charles Eaton,
Woodbury, Connecticut

147. CIRCUS. 1967. Oil on canvas, 30 x 45″.
Kennedy Galleries, Inc., New York City

148. MINEHEAD: IN MEMORY OF ZOLA'S GERMINAL. 1966. Oil on canvas, 50 x 71″.
Kennedy Galleries, Inc., New York City

149. PICNIC. 1967.
Oil on canvas, 46 x 92".
Kennedy Galleries, Inc.,
New York City

150. WHAT'S THE WEATHER GOING TO BE? c. 1965. Oil on canvas, 35 x 25″.
Collection Dr. and Mrs. Arthur B. Coltman, Meadowbrook, Pennsylvania

151. STILL LIFE WITH HORNETS
AND CROCUSES. 1967.
Oil on canvas, 20 x 16″.
Kennedy Galleries, Inc.,
New York City

CHRONOLOGY

1901   October 26: born New York City, son of Miles Evergood. (Meyer Evergood Blashki) and Flora Jane (Perry) Evergood.

1905   Began to take piano lessons from Mme. Rabagliatti. Played in concert with her three years later.

1907–8   Attended the Ethical Culture School.

1909   To England with his mother. Attended various boarding schools there. Spent vacations with his grandmother in London and with other members of his mother's family.

1914   Graduated from Stubbington House School. Passed his written examinations for the Royal Naval Training College, Osborne. Hospitalized for five months with acute appendicitis and gave up naval career. His father and mother, who had joined him in England, changed their name legally from Blashki to Evergood.

1915–19   Attended Eton. Made many Biblical, allegorical, and historical drawings.

1919   Graduated from Eton. To Belgium where he was tutored in French, Latin, and mathematics. Admitted to Trinity Hall College, Cambridge University.

1921   Decided to become an artist. Left Cambridge. Entered the Slade School in London where he studied drawing under Henry Tonks and sculpture with Havard Thomas.

1922   After a visit to Paris made a brief trip to America to settle his parents, who had returned permanently.

1923   Graduated from the Slade School. Rejoined his family in New York. Studied drawing at the Art Students League for a year under William von Schlegell and George Luks. Sketched at night at the Educational Alliance School and did a little painting on his own. Learned etching from Philip Reisman and Harry Sternberg.

1924   Trip to Europe with Melville Chater, writer for the *National Geographic Magazine*. Then to Paris where he had a studio in the Rue du Cherche-Midi. Studied briefly with Jean-Paul Laurens at the Académie Julian, and with André Lhote. Worked independently for a year. Met his future wife, Julia Cross, who was studying painting and ballet. A still life, submitted by his mother, accepted by the National Academy of Design, New York.

1925   Fall: exhibited etching at the Salon d'Automne. Traveled in Italy. Studied for about six weeks at the British Academy in Rome. Then spent several months painting in the South of France.

1926   Returned to America. Continued to paint in a studio in Martinsville, New Jersey, lent to him by the author Harvey O'Higgins.

1927   Death of his mother. Joined group of young artists at the Dudensing Galleries. Given his first one-man show at the Galleries in November.

1929   The Montross Gallery became his dealer.

1930   To France. Had a studio in the Rue Delambre in Paris. Worked independently. Supported himself by working as a carpenter, building stage scenery and as a sparring partner for professional boxers. Studied engraving for a short time with William Hayter at Atelier 17.

1931   To Spain for six months. Studied the work of El Greco, Goya, and Velásquez. Worked for several months in Paris, then returned to America. Married Julia Cross in New York. Both worked for a time in Amelia White's Gallery of American Indian Art.

1934   Exhibited in Whitney Museum's Second Biennial and included in its subsequent Annuals. Joined Public Works of Art Project. Worked for this and its successor, the Federal Art Project of the WPA, until about 1937.

1935   Joined the Midtown Gallery group, New York.

c. 1936   Moved to Woodside, New York.

1936   Took part in the "219 Strike" instituted by two hundred and nineteen artists to protest layoffs from the Federal Art Project. Assigned to Mural Section of the Federal Art Project.

1936–37   On faculty of the American Artists School. Donated his time teaching creative composition and painting.

1937   Joined the A.C.A. Gallery, New York. Completed his mural, *The Story of Richmond Hill*, executed for the public library at Richmond Hill, New York. June: in two-man exhibition with his father at the Athenaeum Gallery, Melbourne, Australia. His painting, *Art on the Beach*, bought by public subscription and presented to the National Gallery of Victoria, in Melbourne.

1938   January: death of his father at Kalorama, Victoria, Australia. Painted mural, *Cotton from Field to Mill*, for the U.S. Post Office in Jackson, Georgia, commissioned by the Section of Fine Arts of the Treasury Department. November: appointed Managing Supervisor, Easel Division of the New York WPA Art Project.

1940   Resident Artist, Kalamazoo College, Michigan, for two years. From this time on represented in virtually every important annual and biennial in the country.

1941   Summer: in hospital for four months after serious operation for cancer. Completed mural, *The Bridge to Life*, for Kalamazoo College.

1942–43   Taught once a week at Muhlenberg College in Allentown, Pennsylvania. Gave private classes in Bethlehem and at the Settlement Music School, Philadelphia.

1943   February: accepted invitation by the War Department (with ten other artists) to make a pictorial record of the war. Gave up his teaching jobs, but was rejected by the Army in May. Found a job at the Midtown Frame Shop, New York. Sale of nine pictures to Joseph H. Hirshhorn enabled him to leave the shop and return to painting.

1945   Bought a house at 132 Bank Street in New York City and a cottage in Patchogue, Long Island.

1946   Sold Bank Street house. Moved to Patchogue where he remodeled the cottage and added a studio. Taught at The Contemporary School of Art, Brooklyn, and briefly at The Jefferson School, New York.

1952   May: moved to Southbury, Connecticut.

1960   Joined Terry Dintenfass, Inc., New York.

1963   Joined Gallery 63, New York. Moved to Bridgewater, Connecticut.

1965   Joined Hammer Galleries, New York.

1970   Joined Kennedy Galleries, New York.

1973   March 11: died at Bridgewater.

Member of the American Artists Congress. President of the Artists Union, and of the United American Artists. Member of the Artists Committee of Action, the Artists League of America, The American Society of Painters, Sculptors and Gravers, An American Group, The National Society of Mural Painters, Artists Equity Association (founding member), and The National Institute of Arts and Letters.

AWARDS: 1935: M. V. Kohnstamm Prize, Art Institute of Chicago. 1941: Carnegie Corporation Grant. 1942: Carnegie Corporation Grant; Sixth Prize, Metropolitan Museum of Art *Artists for Victory* exhibition. 1944: Second Prize, Pepsi-Cola *Portrait of America* exhibition, New York. 1945: Second Honorable Mention, Carnegie Institute. 1946: Second Prize, Franklin D. Roosevelt Competition, A.C.A. Gallery; William H. Tuthill Prize, Art Institute of Chicago; Alexander Shilling Purchase Award. 1947: Second Prize, La Tausca Art Competition, New York. 1949: American Prize, Hallmark Art Award, New York; Carol H. Beck Gold Medal, Pennsylvania Academy of the Fine Arts; Second Prize, Carnegie Institute. 1951: Second W. A. Clark Prize, Corcoran Gallery of Art; First Prize, First Long Island Art Festival. 1952: First Prize, Terry Art Institute, Miami, Florida. 1955: First Prize, Baltimore Museum of Art, *The Seaport* exhibition. 1956: Grant for Painting, American Academy of

Arts and Letters. 1958: Temple Gold Medal, Pennsylvania Academy of the Fine Arts. 1971: Benjamin Altman (Figure) Prize, 146th Annual Exhibition of the National Academy of Design.

One-man exhibitions: Dudensing Galleries, N. Y., 1927; Montross Gallery, N. Y., 1929, also 1933 and 1935; Balzac Galleries, c. 1932; Hollins College, Virginia (drawings), 1935; Denver Art Museum, 1936; A.C.A. Gallery, N. Y., 1938, also 1940, 1942, 1944, 1946, 1948, 1951, 1953, 1955, 1960, 1961 and 1962 (early paintings); Kalamazoo Institute of Arts, 1940; McDonald Gallery, N. Y. (drawings), 1941; Lehigh University, Pennsylvania (drawings and prints), c. 1943; Norlyst Gallery, N. Y. (childhood drawings), 1948; Kansas State Teachers College, 1953; Garelick's Gallery, Detroit, 1953, also 1955; Allen R. Hite Art Institute, University of Louisville (drawings), 1953; University of Minnesota, Duluth (retrospective), 1955; Newcomb Art School Galleries, Tulane University, Louisiana (drawings), 1957; Iowa State Teachers College (drawings), 1957; Terry Dintenfass, Inc., N. Y. (later paintings) 1961, also 1962; Ross-Talalay Gallery, New Haven, Conn., 1962; Galeria 63, Rome, Italy, 1963; Gallery 63, N. Y., 1964; Hammer Galleries, N. Y., 1967; The Gallery of Modern Art, N. Y., 1969; Kennedy Galleries, N. Y., 1971.

SELECTED BIBLIOGRAPHY

WRITINGS BY EVERGOOD

"The Albrights," *New Masses,* vol. 57 (November 27, 1945), pp. 15–16.

Art Digest, vol. 12 (March 1, 1938), p. 3. Response to editorial on the Coffee–Pepper Bill, in "Comments," by Peyton Boswell.

Art Front, vol. 3 (February, 1937), p. 9. Reply to questionnaire sent to artists of the mural section, Federal Art Project.

"Art in Our Time," *The Educational Leader,* Kansas State Teachers College, vol. 18 (July 1, 1954), pp. 3–19. 7 ills.

"The Artist and the Museum" (Address), *Report of the Third Woodstock Art Conference* (John D. Morse, ed.). New York: American Artists Group, 1951, pp. 51–53.

"Building a New Art School," *Art Front,* vol. 3 (April, 1937), p. 21.

"The Finished Product Should Be Invigorating." In *Painters on Painting* (Eric Protter, ed.). New York: Grosset & Dunlap, 1963, p. 235.

Foreword. *Gillen, Kallem, Neuwirth, Shulman.* New York: A.C.A. Gallery, 1938.

———. *Remo Farruggio.* New York: John Heller Gallery, 1935.

———. *Moses Soyer.* Cleveland and New York: World Publishing, n.d., pp. 12–16 (introduction by Charlotte Willard).

———. *See* Valente under General Works.

"My Vote—and Why," *New Masses,* vol. 53 (October 10, 1944), p. 9.

"Realism or Representationalism Will Never Be Outmoded." In *Painters on Painting* (Eric Protter, ed.), pp. 235–36.

"Should the Nation Support Its Art?," *Direction,* vol. 1 (April, 1938), pp. 2–5.

"Social Art: Its Background," *American Contemporary Art.* New York: A.C.A. Gallery, vol. 1 (November, 1944), pp. 3–5.

"Social Surrealism?," *New Masses,* vol. 54 (February 13, 1945), p. 22.

Statement. "Philip Evergood." New York: A.C.A. Gallery, 1962, n.p. 3 ills. *See* A.C.A. under Exhibition Catalogues.

"Sure, I'm a Social Painter," *Magazine of Art,* vol. 36 (November, 1943), pp. 254–59. 8 ills.

"William Gropper," *New Masses,* vol. 50 (February 29, 1944), pp. 26–27.

GENERAL WORKS

Baur, John I. H. "Philip Evergood." In *New Art in America* (John I. H. Baur, ed.). Greenwich, Conn.: New York Graphic Society, in cooperation with Frederick A. Praeger, New York, 1957, pp. 113–17. 5 ills.

———. *Philip Evergood.* New York: Frederick A. Praeger, for the Whitney Museum of American Art, 1960, 125pp. 91 ills.

———. *Revolution and Tradition in Modern American Art.* Cambridge, Mass.: Harvard University Press, 1951, pp. 20, 42. 1 ill.

Beizer, Samuel. "Evergood." In *Art U.S.A. Now* (Lee Nordness, ed., introductory text by Allen S. Weller). Vol. 1. Lucerne: C. J. Bucher, distributed by Viking Press, New York, 1962, pp. 106–9 (including statement by the artist).

Bryant, Edward. "Evergood." In *Doris Caesar/Philip Evergood.* Hartford, Conn.: Wadsworth Atheneum, 1960, pp. 18–24 (including quotations from the artist). 8 ills.

Canaday, John. "On Innocence: With Reference to Philip Evergood" (reprinted from *The New York Times,* May 1, 1960 and *The New York Times Book Review,* July 17, 1960), in *Embattled Critic.* New York: Farrar, Straus & Giroux, 1962, pp. 158–62. 1 ill.

Flanagan, George A. *Understand and Enjoy Modern Art.* Rev. ed. New York: Thomas Y. Crowell, 1962, p. 311.

Gardner, Albert Ten Eyck, and Brown, Milton W. *The New York Painter: A Century of Teaching, Morse to Hofmann.* New York: distributed by New York University Press, New York, 1967, pp. 16, 59, 86, 100. 1 ill.

Genauer, Emily. *Best of Art*. Garden City, N. Y.: Double-day, 1948, pp. 74–76. 3 ills.

Goodrich, Lloyd, and Baur, John I. H. *American Art of Our Century*. New York: Whitney Museum of American Art, 1961, pp. 101–3, 157–58, 163–64, 189, 276, 3 ills.

Larkin, Oliver W. *Art and Life in America*. Rev. ed. New York: Holt, Rinehart & Winston, 1960, pp. 408, 424–25, 430, 437–41, 461, 480, 484. 1 ill.

————. *20 Years* [of] *Evergood*. New York: A.C.A. Gallery, 1946, 108pp (including statement by the artist). 61 ills.

Lippard, Lucy R. *The Graphic Work of Philip Evergood*. New York: Crown Publishers, 1966, 160pp. 177 ills.

Mendelowitz, Daniel M. *A History of American Art*. 2nd ed. New York and Sydney: Holt, Rinehart & Winston, 1970, p. 412. 1 ill.

O'Doherty, Brian. "Philip Evergood." In *Object and Idea: An Art Critic's Journal*. New York: Simon & Schuster, 1967, pp. 62–64 (reprinted from *The New York Times*, May, 1962).

Richardson, E. P. *Painting in America*. Rev. ed. New York: Thomas Y. Crowell, 1965, pp. 405, 410.

Rose, Barbara. *The Twentieth Century*. American Painting, vol. 2. Geneva: Skira, 1969, pp. 42–44. 1 ill.

Time–Life Books, eds. *American Painting 1900–1970*. New York: Time–Life Books, 1970, pp. 9, 93, 98–99, 106–7. 2 ills.

Valente, Alfredo. *Philip Evergood*. South Brunswick, N. J., and New York: A. S. Barnes, 1969, 27pp (foreword by the artist). 65 ills.

EXHIBITION CATALOGUES

A.C.A. Gallery, New York. *Philip Evergood*, 1960. Statements by Elizabeth McCausland and Herman Baron.

————. *Philip Evergood*, 1962. Statement by the artist, foreword by John E. Brown, and statement by Edward Bryant reprinted from *Doris Caesar/Philip Evergood* (*see* Bryant under General Works). 3 ills.

————. *Protest Paintings–U.S.A. 1930–1945*, 1966. Statement by Sidney L. Bergen.

The Brooklyn Museum, New York. *Revolution and Tradition*, text by John I. H. Baur, 1951.

Gallery 63 Inc., New York. *Philip Evergood*, 1964. Statement by Edward Bryant. 6 ills.

The Gallery of Modern Art, New York. *Philip Evergood*, by Alfredo Valente, 1969 (*see* under General Works).

Hammer Galleries, New York. *Philip Evergood*, 1967. Foreword by Victor J. Hammer. 26 ills.

Illinois, University of, Urbana. *Exhibition of Contemporary*

American Painting, 1948, n.p. 1 ill.; 1949, 1 ill.; 1950, p. 172. 1 ill.; 1951, p. 174; 1953, pp. 180–81. 1 ill.; 1955, pp. 196–97. 1 ill.; 1957, pp. 199–200; 1961, pp. 160–61 (quotation from the artist). 1 port. 1 ill.; 1965, p. 139 (statement by the artist). 1 ill.

Marlborough–Gerson Gallery, New York. *The New York Painter*, benefit exhibition for the New York University Art Collection, 1967, pp. 16, 59, 86, 100. 1 ill.

The Museum of Modern Art, New York. *Romantic Painting in America*, text by James Thrall Soby and Dorothy Miller, 1943, pp. 42–43. 1 ill.

Whitney Museum of American Art, New York. *Philip Evergood*, text by John I. H. Baur, 1960. Exhibition circulated to Walker Art Center, Minneapolis, 1960; Wadsworth Atheneum, Hartford, Conn., which produced separate catalogue, 1960 (*see* Bryant under General Works); Des Moines Art Center, 1960; San Francisco Museum of Art, 1960–61; Colorado Springs Fine Arts Center, 1961; Munson–Williams–Proctor Institute, Utica, N. Y., 1961 (*see* Baur under General Works).

PERIODICALS

"Big Spender," *Time*, vol. 66 (July 25, 1955), p. 72. 2 ills.

Blomshield, John. "Philip Evergood," *'47 the Magazine of the Year*, vol. 1 (June, 1947), pp. 140–45. 4 ills.

Brown, Gordon. "An Interview with Philip Evergood," *Art Voices from Around the World*, vol. 2 (December, 1963), pp. 3, 8–9, cover. 1 port. 5 ills.

B[rown], G[ordon]. "Philip Evergood," *Art Voices from Around the World*, vol. 3 (June, 1964), p. 9, cover. 1 ill.

Brown, Gordon. "Philip Evergood; At the Gallery of Modern Art," *Arts Magazine*, vol. 43 (May, 1969), p. 51. 3 ills.

Burger, William Thor. "Evergood: Pioneering a New Art," *New Masses*, vol. 59 (May 21, 1946), pp. 7–9. 1 ill.

C[ampbell], L[awrence]. "Philip Evergood," *Art News*, vol. 63 (Summer, 1964), p. 16. 1 ill.

————. "Philip Evergood, Umberto Romano," *Art News*, vol. 63 (February, 1965), p. 19.

Canaday, John. "Some Views of the Artist," *The New York Times Book Review*, July 17, 1960, pp. 7, 29. 2 ills.

Carline, Richard. "Fine Art in Modern America," *Studio*, vol. 120 (September, 1940), pp. 69, 73, 74. 1 ill.

Chikadiev, A. A critical article on the work of Philip Evergood, translated by David Burliuk and Julia Evergood. *Art of the U.S.A.*, Rockwell Kent, ed. Moscow, 1960.

C[ooper], S[helby]. "Philip Evergood," *Art News*, vol. 61 (Summer, 1962), p. 46. 1 ill.

Dennison, George. "Month in Review," *Arts,* vol. 34 (May, 1960), pp. 50–53. 5 ills. Reprinted as "Philip Evergood: A Retrospective View," in *Arts Yearbook 6* (James R. Mellow, ed.). 1962, pp. 112–14. 1 ill.

Dunham, Alice. "The Courage of Philip Evergood," *Mainstream,* vol. 13 (June, 1960), pp. 56–60.

"Ever Great Evergood," *Newsweek,* vol. 23 (March 27, 1944), pp. 93–94.

"Evergood, Born Satirist," *Art Digest,* vol. 12 (March, 1938), p. 26.

"Evergood To Show Art Work In Exhibit Previewing Today," *New Haven Register* [New Haven, Conn.], October 21, 1962. 1 port.

"Evergood's Art Expands," *Art Digest,* vol. 7 (April 1, 1933), p. 16.

"Evergood's Lusty Mural Stirs Citizen Wrath," *Art Digest,* vol. 12 (June 1, 1938), p. 18. 1 ill.

Farber, Manny. "57th Street and Thereabouts," *Magazine of Art,* vol. 35 (November, 1942), pp. 261, 269. 1 ill.

Frankenstein, Alfred. "Philip Evergood Is a One-Picture Painter," *San Francisco Chronicle,* December 11, 1960. 2 ills.

G[enauer], E[mily]. "Whitney's Evergood Solo Show Excellent," *New York Herald Tribune,* April 10, 1960. Section P, p. 7.

Gibbs, Joe. "Philip Evergood Looks Across Twenty Years," *Art Digest,* vol. 20 (April 15, 1946), pp. 9, 30. 1 ill.

Gottlieb, Harry. "The Miner. Eight Drawings by Philip Evergood," *Mainstream,* vol. 1 (Fall, 1947), pp. 452–60. 8 ills.

Louchheim, Aline B. "Evergood and the War," *Art News,* vol. 43 (March 15, 1944), p. 16. 1 ill.

McBride, Henry. "Philip Evergood Relaxes," *Art News,* vol. 50 (April, 1951), p. 49. 1 ill.

McCausland, Elizabeth. "The Plastic Organization of Philip Evergood," *Parnassus,* vol. 11 (March, 1939), pp. 19–21. 3 ills.

Michaelson, Charles. "Philip Evergood: Artist of the People," *RWDSU Record,* vol. 7 (July 17, 1960), p. 13. 1 port. 1 ill.

"More In Sorrow," *Time,* vol. 75 (April 18, 1960), pp. 92–93. 1 port. 1 ill.

Oglesby, John C. "Evergood Retrospective Opens in SF Museum of Art," *Sacramento Bee* [Sacramento, Calif.], December 11, 1960. 3 ills.

"Pepsi-Cola Hits the Paint," *Newsweek,* vol. 24 (July 31, 1944), p. 62.

"Philip Evergood Evaluated Pro and Con," *Art Digest,* vol. 14 (April 1, 1940), p. 20. 1 ill.

"Philip Evergood Wades In," *Art Digest,* vol. 9 (February 1, 1935), p. 16.

"Philip Evergood When He Is Good—and Bad," *Art Digest,* vol. 17 (November 1, 1942), p. 9. 1 ill.

Porter, Fairfield. "Evergood Paints a Picture," *Art News,* vol. 50 (January, 1952), pp. 30–33, 55–56. 9 ills.

"Proving Polemics and Humor Mix," *Art News,* vol. 45 (May, 1946), p. 35.

R[eed], J[udith] K[aye]. "Not So Evergood," *Art Digest,* vol. 22 (April 15, 1948), p. 11.

R[iley], M[aude]. "Philip Evergood's Slant on the War," *Art Digest,* vol. 18 (March 15, 1944), p. 17. 1 ill.

Salpeter, Harry. "About Philip Evergood," *Coronet,* vol. 2 (May 1, 1937), pp. 174–75. 1 ill.

Schiff, Bennett. "In the Galleries," *New York Post,* April 10, 1960, Magazine, p. 10. 1 ill.

Seckler, Dorothy Gees. "Seven Major Retrospectives," *Art in America,* vol. 47 (Winter, 1959), p. 102. 1 ill.

S[imon], R[ita]. "Philip Evergood," *Arts Magazine,* vol. 43 (Summer, 1969), p. 55. 1 ill.

T[horp], C[harlotte]. "Philip Evergood," *Arts Magazine,* vol. 41 (March, 1967), p. 60.

Tworkov, Jack. "Philip Evergood," *New York Artist,* vol. 1 (April, 1940), p. 3. 1 ill.

Tyler, Betty. "Realistic Art of Philip Evergood Dramatizes Passionate Convictions," *Bridgeport Sunday Post* [Bridgeport, Conn.], August 7, 1966, pp. C–3, C–8. 1 port. 6 ills.

W[hite], C[laire] N[icolas]. "Philip Evergood," *Art News,* vol. 66 (April, 1967), p. 10.

Wlaschin, Ken. "From Rome," *Art Voices from Around the World,* vol. 2 (November, 1963), p. 18.

INDEX

PHOTOGRAPH CREDITS

The following numbers refer to plate numbers.